Digital Evolution
Security & Facts
about
Cloud, Internet of Things
&
5G
Technologies

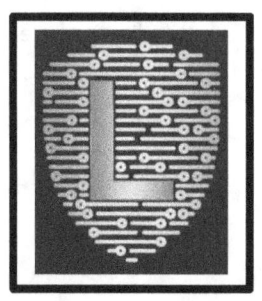

Copyright © All rights reserved worldwide.

YOUR RIGHTS: This book is restricted to your personal use only. It does not come with any other rights.

LEGAL DISCLAIMER: This book is protected by international copyright law and may not be copied, reproduced, given away, or used to create derivative works without the publisher's expressed permission. The publisher retains full copyrights to this book.

The author has made every reasonable effort to be as accurate and complete as possible in the creation of this book and to ensure that the information provided is free from errors; however, the author/publisher/ reseller assumes no responsibility for errors, omissions, or contrary interpretation of the subject matter herein and does not warrant or represent at any time that the contents within are accurate due to the rapidly changing nature of the Internet.

Any perceived slights of specific persons, peoples, or organizations are unintentional.

The purpose of this book is to educate and there are no guarantees of income, sales, or results implied. The publisher/author/reseller can therefore not be held accountable for any poor results you may attain when implementing the techniques or when following any guidelines set out for you in this book.

Any product, website, and company names mentioned in this book are the trademarks or copyright properties of their respective owners. The author/publisher/reseller is not associated or affiliated with them in any way. Nor does the referred product, website, and company names sponsor, endorse, or approve this product.

COMPENSATION DISCLOSURE: Unless otherwise explicitly stated, you should assume that the links contained in this book may be affiliate links, and the author/publisher/reseller may earn a commission if you click on them and buy the product/service mentioned in this book. However, the author/publisher/reseller disclaims any liability that may result from your involvement with any such websites/products. You should perform due diligence before buying mentioned products or services.

This constitutes the entire license agreement. Any disputes or terms not discussed in this agreement are at the sole discretion of the publisher.

Acknowledgement:

Many thanks to my family for their support throughout the researching and writing of this book.

"My help comes from the Lord, who made heaven and earth."

(Psalms 121:2)

Food for thought

Each business is a victim of Digital Darwinism, the evolution of consumer behaviour when society and technology evolve faster than the ability to exploit it. Digital Darwinism does not discriminate. Every business is threatened.

— **Brian Solis**

Contents

Acknowledgement: _____ 3

Food for thought _____ 4

Abstract _____ 9

Overview _____ 10

Chapter One _____ 12

Introduction _____ 12

Chapter Two _____ 18

Cloud Computing _____ 18

    Reasons for Migrating to the Cloud _____ 19
        Improved Security _____ 20
        Cost Reduction _____ 20
        Mobile Access _____ 20
        Rethink Password Access _____ 20
        Flexibility _____ 21
        Reliability _____ 21

    Cloud Computing Models _____ 22
        Private Cloud: _____ 22
        Public Cloud: _____ 22
        Hybrid Cloud: _____ 23
        Community Cloud _____ 25

    Service Types _____ 25
        Infrastructure as a Service (IaaS) _____ 25
        Platform as a Service (PaaS) _____ 25
        Software as a Service (SaaS) _____ 25

    Zero-Trust Policy _____ 26

    Device Enrolment _____ 26

    Virtualisation _____ 26

    Fog or Edge Computing _____ 26

    Compare and Contrast: _____ 28

    Cloud Computing Models _____ 29

    Cloud Security Issues _____ 30
        Data Breaches _____ 30
        Impacts of Cloud Misconfiguration _____ 30
        Data Security Strategies _____ 31

Chapter Three _____ 33

Internet of Things (IoT) _____ 33

5 Areas of IoT 35
Perception 35
Network 35
Middleware 35
Application 35
Business 35

IoT Benefits 36
Sharing Medical Data 36
Team Collaboration 36
Cost Savings 36
Predictive Maintenance 36
Supply Chain Management 36

IoT Disadvantages 37
Internet Connectivity 37
Limited Storage 37
Data Privacy & Security 37

Barriers Preventing IoT Adoption 38

Integrating Cloud Computing with IoT 39

How IoT is Complemented by Cloud Computing 41
Storage capabilities 41
Communication capabilities 41
Data Security 41
Data Privacy 42
Interoperability 43
Energy Consumption 43
Resource allocation 43
Identity and Access management 43

Chapter Four 44

5th Generation Networks (5G) 44

Brief History of Telecommunication 46
What Makes a Network 5G? 47
5G Early Development Rollouts 47

5G Services 49

Fixed-Wireless Access (FWA) 50

5G Attributes 50
Handover Process 50
Quality of Service 51
Signal Strength 51
Deployment strategy 51

5G vs 4G	51
Enhanced Mobile Broadband	52
Ultra-Reliable and Low Latency Communications	52
5G	53
Network Slicing	56
Network Slicing Service Requirements:	58
5G Disadvantages:	60
Lack of Availability	60
5G Incompatibility	61
New Security Issues	61
High Capital Expenditure	61
Lack of Backwards Compatibility	61
Unknown Risks with Technology in Infancy	61
High Training Resources	61
Manufacturing Cost & Sale Price	62
Chapter Five	63
Integration of the Cloud & 5G Network	63
Integration Advantages	66
Businesses and the Cloud	66
Cloud with 5G Performance	66
Processing Power & Speed	66
Cost Reduction	66
Network and System Updates	66
Independent Smart Devices	67
Edge Computing	68
Enhance Virtual Reality and Augmented Reality	68
Integration Disadvantages	68
Chapter Six	70
Integration of the Cloud, IoT & 5G	70
Security and Issues	72
Matrix of different factors of the technologies – Table 1	74
Integration of the 3 Technologies– Table 2	77
Chapter Seven	79
Conclusions	79
Recommendations	85
References:	87
Appendices:	91

Appendix A: Cloud Frequently Asked Questions (FAQ) 92

How do I know the level of data security in any cloud environment? 92
When is the best time to migrate to the cloud environment? 92
How do you pay for the cloud services? 92
Can an organisation migrate all their business operations and data to the cloud? 92
How do I determine how much cloud memory is sufficient for my data? 94
How do I make sure that my password is safe to use? 94
How do I determine which volumes of my data to store in the cloud? 95
How do I determine the best cloud environment for me? 95
How do I protect my information when communicating from an intelligent device via the 5G network? 95
How do I confirm whether or not my cloud supplier is a third party? 95
How do I confirm the location of where my data is stored? 95
In the event of a breach of my cloud environment, who is liable? 96
How do I confirm whether the cost of using the cloud environment is reasonable? 96
Is it better to carry out online transactions (e.g. financial transactions) via a mobile device or laptop when using cloud data? 96
Which companies are the top hybrid cloud providers? 97
Amazon provides cloud services for which organisations? 99
What examples could you give on cloud misconfiguration? 99
Where could you find the list of companies whose data or environment have been compromised? 99
What is the best viable in-premises cloud storage? (Tech Republic) 99
Who benefits from Google Cloud Platform (GCP)? 99
What products make up a sample Cloud Platform? 101

Appendix B: 5G Frequently Asked Questions (FAQ) 102

Is it secure to use 5G network for sensitive or private data? 102
What is Augmented Reality or AR? 102
What is Virtual Reality or VR? 102
Which company first introduced virtualization technology and what was the name at the time? 102
What is Network Slicing in relation to 5G networks? 102
What is a campus network? 103
Why are Chinese technology companies like Huawei being prevented from working on the 5G network in the United States and Britain's 5G infrastructure? 103

Appendix C: Acronym Glossary 104

Index: 106

Abstract

Cloud computing, Internet of Things (IoT) and 5th Generation (5G) technologies play a pivotal role in our society today. The implementation of these technologies at large will continue to play a part in more ways than one in data management.

This book will focus on the facts about various aspects of the three technologies individually and when integrated. Issues or challenges that exist within each one will be presented, as well as existing challenges when integrated and the likely or available solutions.

This book will serve as a guide to provide some information about these three technologies for those interested small businesses and tech professionals.

Efforts will be made to ensure diagrammatic representation of the various technologies are presented in order to further clarify the make-up of each one of them and when integrated.

The diagrams are also essential to further clarify the workings of each of the technologies as a single entity or as integrated systems. Like the saying, a picture paints a thousand words. It is expected that the readers will have a better understanding of both the technical and non-technical aspects of the book.

In the appendices, a list of frequently asked questions and important points will be covered. Basically, this is to provide additional information on any of the topics covered in this book and to serve as a basic knowledge base.

The content of this book was compiled after months of research work, from technical books with related topics, digital network magazines, research reports, mobile survey reports, data centre reports (for Cisco, AWS, IBM, Google, etc.), 1-2-1 short interviews with security professionals and materials from cyber security conferences.

Overview

At the time of writing this book, it is apparent that most personal and business use of information technology (IT) begins with suggestions or advice from experts without personal technical understanding. Subsequently, individuals lack practical knowledge on the impact on their businesses if things go wrong or when the technology is not applied correctly. It is like when you purchase the latest phone on the market because you've been advised that you could use it as a mobile office. Due to your limited knowledge, you are unlikely to know how to use most of the functions or what to do when something goes wrong.

Cloud computing, Internet of Things (IoT) and 5th Generation (5G) technologies have a future of growth and opportunities to change the business world. Millions of people and businesses make use of the cloud to store their data and process important transactions. However, most of them do not understand the limitations of using the cloud and the appropriate cloud technology to use. The use of the cloud environment is not free and sometimes it may not be the best option.

The Internet of Things is still new to most people even though the technology has been around for several years. Some businesses understand the importance of the technology, however, in terms of cyber security, still lack the level of knowledge needed to limit the risks and threats associated with the use of IoT devices.

The 5G mobile technology is new, and the key message being presented by the providers is that it will revolutionise the world, especially the mobile telecommunication industry. When compared to the 1st through to 4th generation networks, 5G is a huge leap and is likely to galvanise most business operations.

The exciting thing is that combining these three technologies can work to improve most business operations. To understand the effective logistics of the technologies, one must also understand the hidden risks associated with them.

This book will provide facts about cloud computing, Internet of Things and 5G mobile technology. The information will not cover everything, because, in the digital age, most technologies will continue to evolve and new things will be introduced in the future.

The idea of this book is to highlight the importance of each technology, its benefits and problems. It will also highlight the benefits and problems associated with them when they are integrated.

A chapter will be dedicated to important questions and answers which would improve the knowledge of individuals and businesses when making use of any of these technologies.

Chapter One

Introduction

> ... Emphasis will be placed on security risks and threats. Also the solutions to mitigate or prevent the risks and threats will be provided...

To ensure that every reader benefits from at least some aspects of this book, if not all, a chapter will deal with the facts about each of the three technologies separately and then the integrations of all three.

The main objective is to present the importance of each of the technologies to consumers and businesses whilst explaining features, benefits and shortcomings. Emphasis will be placed on security risks and threats. Also, the solutions to mitigate or prevent the risks and threats will be provided.

The figure below represents the integration of each one of the three technologies with one another and their security levels.

- S1 – security level when cloud and IoT devices are integrated
- S2 – security level when IoT devices and 5G are integrated
- S3 – security level when cloud and 5G are integrated
- S0 – the security level when the three are integrated.

This is an opportunity to look at how secure our data, systems and networks are when we combine these technologies.

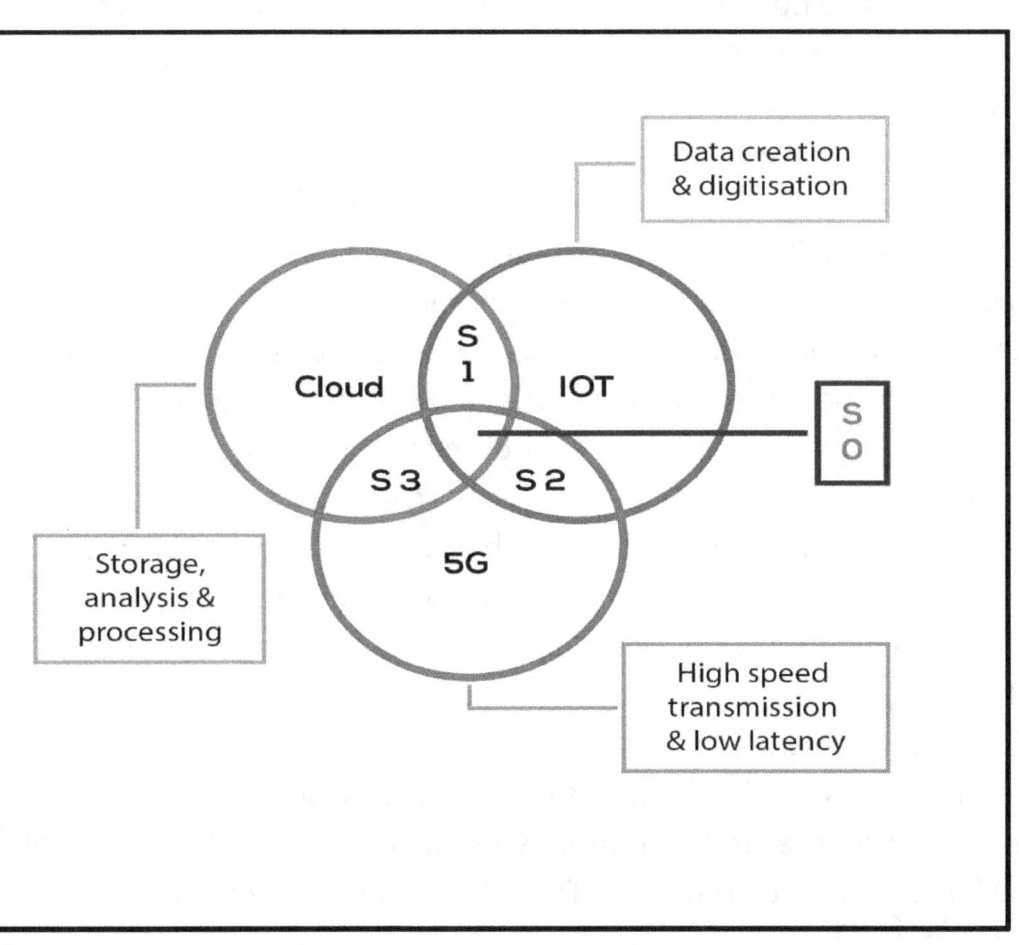

In the appendices, there will be information comprising of frequently asked questions and acronyms with their meaning.

Figure 1 below shows the strategy applied, to ensure that all the required topics were covered according to the scope of this book.

Cloud computing will cover the types available on the market at the time of writing this book and their differences. Due to the increase in uptake by businesses, security issues will be highlighted.

Improving the readers' level of knowledge and understanding of any of the technologies will enable them to make informed business or personal decisions, if and when necessary. In terms of cloud computing, new or medium-sized businesses will be able to ask the right questions from cloud providers before or once they have decided to migrate their data to the cloud environment.

This book couldn't have been written at a better time than during the catastrophic impact caused by the coronavirus or Covid-19 pandemic, which ravaged every part of the globe. In a matter of days, hundreds to thousands of people were killed and businesses were shut down, people were locked down to reduce the transmission and spread of the virus. This meant that the use of available technologies to enable some key businesses and facilities to continue to operate became apparent. Internet transactions increased significantly, new technologies to enhance communication were at the forefront of business priorities, there was high demand for digital storage or cloud facilities and the importance of data security couldn't be overemphasised.

The panic to prevent the spread of the virus and at the same time maintain business continuity meant that some security policies became unfit for purpose due to change in the working environment and a surge in the use of untested devices or tools. This led to high cyber attacks because systems and devices became vulnerable and could easily be compromised. For example, some office staff were now working from home with their desktops which were originally configured to be used within their more secure office network. Also, the flexibility of using both business and personal emails for business communications became a non-issue temporarily but with a high-risk tag.

This pandemic has changed the way businesses operate and how humans will interact in the future forever. Most businesses and even those that didn't think it was possible, are now run remotely. There is hunger for the next best technology that would improve or enhance working remotely and at the same time provide data security when in-situ or in-transit.

Although a high percentage of people in the world now know that 5G is being rolled out, most people do not understand what it will provide, and most will continue to use 4G if it works for them. Some people even thought that the 5G rollout was the cause of the coronavirus transmission. The content of this book will help some business leaders think ahead of ways to plan and improve their business operations in order to maintain a fair lead over their competitors where necessary.

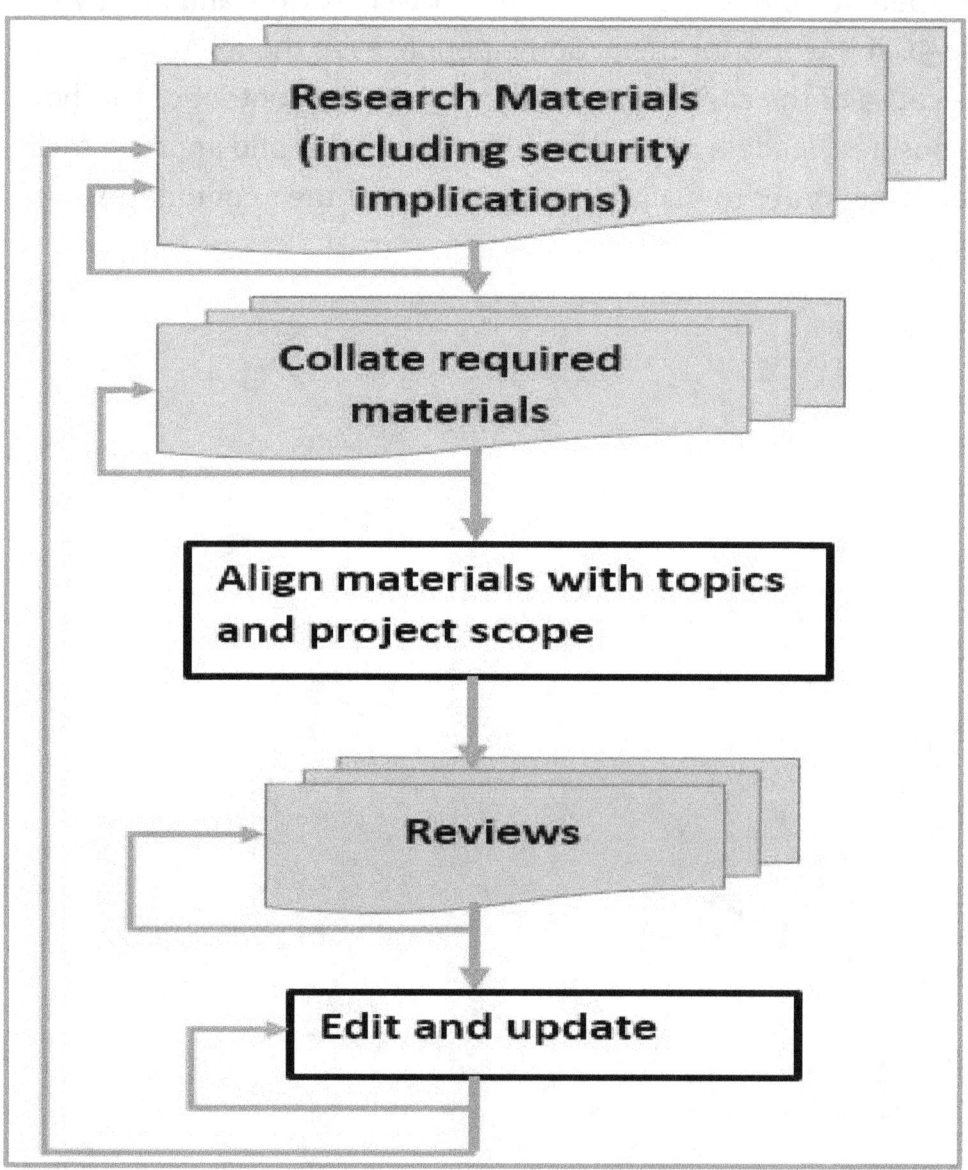

Fig 1: Strategy applied in order to write this book

Gathering appropriate materials for this book was challenging, but from the sources available, it was apparent that people spend a lot of money and time on their mobile devices but are not aware of how to secure them effectively. In other words, they are not security conscious and could become the weakest link in their organisation, especially where most organisations allow you to bring your own devices to work. Hopefully, this book will help the reader to start to think more about security in any environment they find themselves. When purchasing digital devices or products, keeping your data secure should take precedence.

Chapter Two
Cloud Computing

... To ensure that a secure cloud environment is designed and implemented, focus is placed on key areas of cloud security solutions; Confidentiality, integrity, availability of data and system infrastructure ...

For some years now, there has been increased interest in the use of cloud computing by organisations in order to reduce the cost of acquiring or updating their IT infrastructure, software costs and improving operating speed by relying on 3rd party organisations or cloud environment providers. However, the adoption of these models of operation has introduced security concerns, which traditional IT solutions cannot resolve. This means that new and improved solutions are needed to deal with these risks and threats as they develop.

Cloud computing is the on-demand availability of computer system resources, especially data storage (**cloud storage**) and computing power, accessible via the internet, without direct active management by the user. (Wikipedia, 2020)

Rather than keeping files on a proprietary hard drive or local storage device, cloud-based storage makes it possible to save them to a remote database. As long as an electronic device has access to the web, it has access to the data and the software programs to run it. (Investopedia, 2020).
Cloud computing is a popular option for people and businesses for a number of reasons including cost savings, increased productivity, speed and efficiency, performance, and security. (Investopedia, 2020).

To ensure that a secure cloud environment is designed and implemented, the focus is placed on key areas of cloud security solutions; confidentiality, integrity, availability of data (i.e. when in transit or storage), and system infrastructure.

Reasons for Migrating to the Cloud

Migrating to the cloud environment may not be for some individuals and businesses at a given time. However, once it has been decided to make this move, there are some security practices which should be considered or adopted. This is particular to the mobile cloud model which introduces a different network defence than the traditional firewall defence.

Migrating an organisation's databases to the cloud is another important decision that most organisations have to make and there are good reasons for going this way.
The points to consider are the following;

Improved Security

This is possible due to the high level of security knowledge and resources available within the cloud environment. The provider must ensure that the required level of testing is carried out and regular updates are done when needed. The number of activities required to maintain a secure environment cannot be successfully done by most organisations within their premises.

Cost Reduction

The cost of ensuring cloud security maintenance is one of the numerous savings realised by many organisations. They will also be free from database operating, maintenance, updating, patching and installing costs. It shouldn't however be forgotten that there are other costs which are associated with migrating databases into the cloud, like licensing and subscription charges. Also indirect costs like loss of revenue due to unexpected application downtime, loss of customer data during outages and charges of network usage during the migration. Even with these initial costs, organisations do end up with good levels of savings overall.

Mobile Access

Unlike traditional methods of accessing data in any organisation by use of desktop, laptops via a traditional secure defence, cloud computing has introduced the flexibility of allowing data accessibility using our mobiles or handsets from any part of the globe. This creates its own security problems due to the inability of the traditional wall of defence to cope with a variety of threats and unauthorised intrusions.

Rethink Password Access

It is a fact that a high volume of people's login details are stolen daily. The majority of people recycle their login details across several applications, which makes this a bigger problem when you consider the number of applications involved within the cloud environment. An alternative access method to consider could be multi-factor authentication. Imagine whenever you are about to login to a system, you will require your password and then a code will be sent to your mobile device as the second information needed to grant you access. This would make a significant difference because even if your passwords fall in the wrong hands, the intruder would still need to be in possession of your mobile device before access could be granted. Which improves the safety of your data and systems.

Flexibility

The cloud environment provides the capability for organisations to either scale up or down, if and when required. This is something that is not possible to do within physical premises because any appliance, device or software required will need time to be installed or developed. However, the resources are already available within the cloud and it would be a matter of increasing or reducing whatever is needed without any delay.

Reliability

This is one aspect of the cloud that makes a huge difference to customers. This is made possible by the highly skilled administrators that work in the cloud centres to ensure the day to day operations of the environment. Lack of reliable database access will impact heavily on business revenue and loss of customers.

Cloud Computing Models

There are four main types of cloud computing services, with different characteristics.
They are Private Cloud, Public Cloud, Hybrid Cloud and Community Cloud.

Private Cloud:

Private clouds are typically adopted by large organisations that deploy the cloud technology within their premises or rely on a third-party organisation to supply a dedicated cloud environment for an establishment. The benefit of this cloud type is that they have full control of how the cloud environment is accessed and can prevent unauthorised access. The processes and services are protected by the company's firewall and its installed intrusion detection system. More often than not, these establishments are aware of the location of their stored data and are capable of encrypting either their transit or non-transit data by using their preferred and tested encryption software. They are able to classify some data as high or medium risks which require protection, and some as low risks which may not affect their business if they fall into the wrong hands. The high and medium risks data are likely to be encrypted when in storage or when they are being sent to a different location.
Organisations with this private cloud environment are able to apply their provisioning processes, software and security upgrades flexibly without delay because decisions are made internally. With the private cloud, these organisations have the required skills to maintain security compliance, auditing and business operations.

Looking at figure 2 (i.e. Cloud Computing Models Diagram) below, the private cloud computing is represented by the blue rectangle. The diagram shows the three levels (i.e. infrastructure, platform, applications) which make up any private cloud environment deployed. The environment could be accessed from tablets, laptops or phones via an internet connection. An example of an organisation with private cloud computing is VMware's vSphere.

Public Cloud:

Large organisations or enterprises use this cloud environment as the platform to provide IT with flexibility, agility and the required scalability. They are able to expedite digital initiatives due to these capabilities, including the ability to accommodate most future and emerging technologies. For example, artificial intelligence (AI), Big Data & Analytics, etc.

However, it is a known fact that large organisations are faced with problems when migrating to a public cloud environment. Most of these problems are caused by changes or alterations made to existing processes and tools, migration and managing application. Also not having the required cloud skills to ensure smooth operations within the cloud environment. One of the key benefits of the public cloud is its technological innovation and the access capability of the latest digital innovation which it provides (D Mohan, IDC Analyse the future).

Looking at figure 2 (i.e. Cloud Computing Models Diagram) below, the public cloud computing is represented by the red rectangle. The diagram shows the three levels (i.e. infrastructure, platform, applications) which make up any public cloud environments deployed. However, the environment belongs to a third-party provider. The environment could be accessed from tablets, laptops and phones via an internet connection. However, access is controlled by the third-party organisation and each consumer will pay only for the service they use. An example of an organisation with public cloud computing is Amazon's AWS.

Hybrid Cloud:

Hybrid Cloud computing combines the best parts of the private and public cloud. Organisations or establishments that adopt the hybrid cloud will use the private cloud part to keep and process highly sensitive information or data. However, they will use the public cloud to store and process non-sensitive or generic data. For example, the deployment of the company's website will be placed in the public cloud because access limitation is almost non-existent. Looking at figure 2 (i.e. Cloud Computing Models Diagram) below, hybrid cloud computing is represented by the purple rectangle. The diagram shows the three levels (i.e. infrastructure, platform, applications) which make up any hybrid cloud environments that are deployed. However, the environment shares the private and public cloud which could be provided by a third-party cloud provider. The environment could be accessed from tablets, laptops or phones via internet connection. However, the private cloud side access is controlled by the organisation but the public cloud side access control is controlled by a third-party organisation. Just like the organisation using the public cloud, consumers of the hybrid cloud will pay only for the service they use on the public side of the cloud. There is an element of flexibility in the use of the hybrid cloud because organisations could transfer or move data from the private cloud to the public cloud and vice-versa if the level of sensitivity changes.

A good example of an organisation with a hybrid cloud computing is Microsoft's Azure.

Community Cloud

Community Cloud, as the name suggests, is deployed by third-party organisations for businesses or enterprises with common business operations or processes. For example, financial or educational institutions. Multiple organisations will share their existing infrastructure and resources through the cloud by allowing each other access.

Looking at figure 1 (i.e. Cloud Computing Models Diagram) below, the community cloud computing is represented by the yellow rectangle. The diagram shows the three levels (i.e. infrastructure, platform, applications) which make up any cloud environments that are deployed. However, the cloud environment belongs to a third-party provider. The environment could be accessed from tablets, laptops or phones via internet connection.

An example of an organisation with a community cloud computing is the intelligence agency, etc. Also, some organisations' online cloud communities are being globally powered by a provider like Hivebrite.

Service Types

In cloud computing, there are 3 main service models. They are the following:

Infrastructure as a Service (IaaS)

This is where the user can make use of already provisioned network facilities, storage, operating systems and the level of control is in accordance to the agreement with the cloud provider. For example, Amazon simple storage service or S3, Microsoft Azure and Amazon compute cloud or EC2.

Platform as a Service (PaaS)

This is where the user has the capability to deploy applications, infrastructure or tools onto the cloud, but the level of control is dependent on the agreement with the cloud provider. For example, Microsoft SQL Azure, Amazon Relational Database Service or RDS and Oracle Cloud.

Software as a Service (SaaS)

This is where the user has the capability to use provisioned applications in the cloud according to the agreement with the cloud provider. The user will access the applications through client interfaces like web browsers. For example, Microsoft office 365 and Salesforce.com.

Zero-Trust Policy

Since introducing the mobile cloud computing infrastructure adds to security risks, it is important to take stringent measures like putting in place a security policy which would ensure that every application or device of any user that requires access to your organisation's data are checked thoroughly before permission is granted. In other words, no one must be trusted.

Device Enrolment

Alongside Zero-trust policy, the idea of enrolling all devices should also be introduced within an organisation. This makes it possible for all the contents of any device to be encrypted and furthermore provides the avenue through which regular updates can be applied to any handset. Especially, once an access violation has been committed, the device in question could be temporarily disabled or system access could be denied until all related issues are resolved (Foster, 2019).

Virtualisation

Cloud computing technology stands out due to the adoption of virtualisation in order to maximize processing efficiency. Thus, providing the capability of displaying location independence, flexibility, scalability, broad-network access and resource allocation.

Fog or Edge Computing

With a better understanding of cloud computing and different types of cloud services, it would be a good idea to give a brief introduction to fog or edge computing. This is an important type of cloud computing but from the name, they are useful around the fringes or edges of the network, where communication links are close to the user.

Consider a manufacturing environment with a global presence with system architecture which processes a vast amount of data centrally. Which means, the data is received and sent over a long distance to be used by endpoints on various locations. Depending on what the data is used for at those endpoints would determine how frequently they are needed and sent back to be processed by the central server. The majority of the time, speed is of the essence when you are dealing with operations in areas like machinery, video streaming, medical operation or aviation. As such, for things to work without a problem, there shouldn't be any delay in receiving the required data.

However, due to the distance of data travel and other impacting factors (e.g. time of processing, network congestion and bandwidth) along the way, it is almost impossible for the current technology to deliver streams of data at low latency.

Due to these limitations, the idea to distribute essential data processing closer to the edge of the network or the user was embraced as a good solution going forward. Which means, the end-user is continuously provided the required data when needed and without delay. Cloud computing which is provided at the edge is known as cloudlets or fog.

Compare and Contrast:

Table 2 (below) highlights the similarities and differences between the various forms of cloud computing models.

Characteristics	Private	Public	Hybrid	Community
Virtualization technology	√	√	√	√
Operate via the internet	√	√	√	√
Security risk is very high		√		
Security risk is medium			√	√
Security risk is very low	√			
Application level exist	√	√	√	√
Middle level exist	√	√	√	√
Operating System level exist	√	√	√	√
Hardware level exist	√	√	√	√
Multi-tenancy architecture exist	√	√	√	√
Cloud provider is more in control of resources		√		
Consumer or organisation is more in control of resources	√		√	√
Scalability is always possible	√	√	√	√
Cloud provider is responsible for all systems configuration, provisioning and patching		√	√	√
Auditability is essential	√	√	√	√
Use of automation to reduce complexity	√	√	√	√
Cloud providers are knowledgeable in cloud security and risk levels	√	√	√	√
Some on-premises hardware is likely	√		√	√
Location of infrastructure may not be known		√		

Table 2: Characteristics of the four types of cloud computing models

Figure 2 (below) provides a high-level view of the different types of cloud computing environments as described in the section above.

Cloud Computing Models Diagram

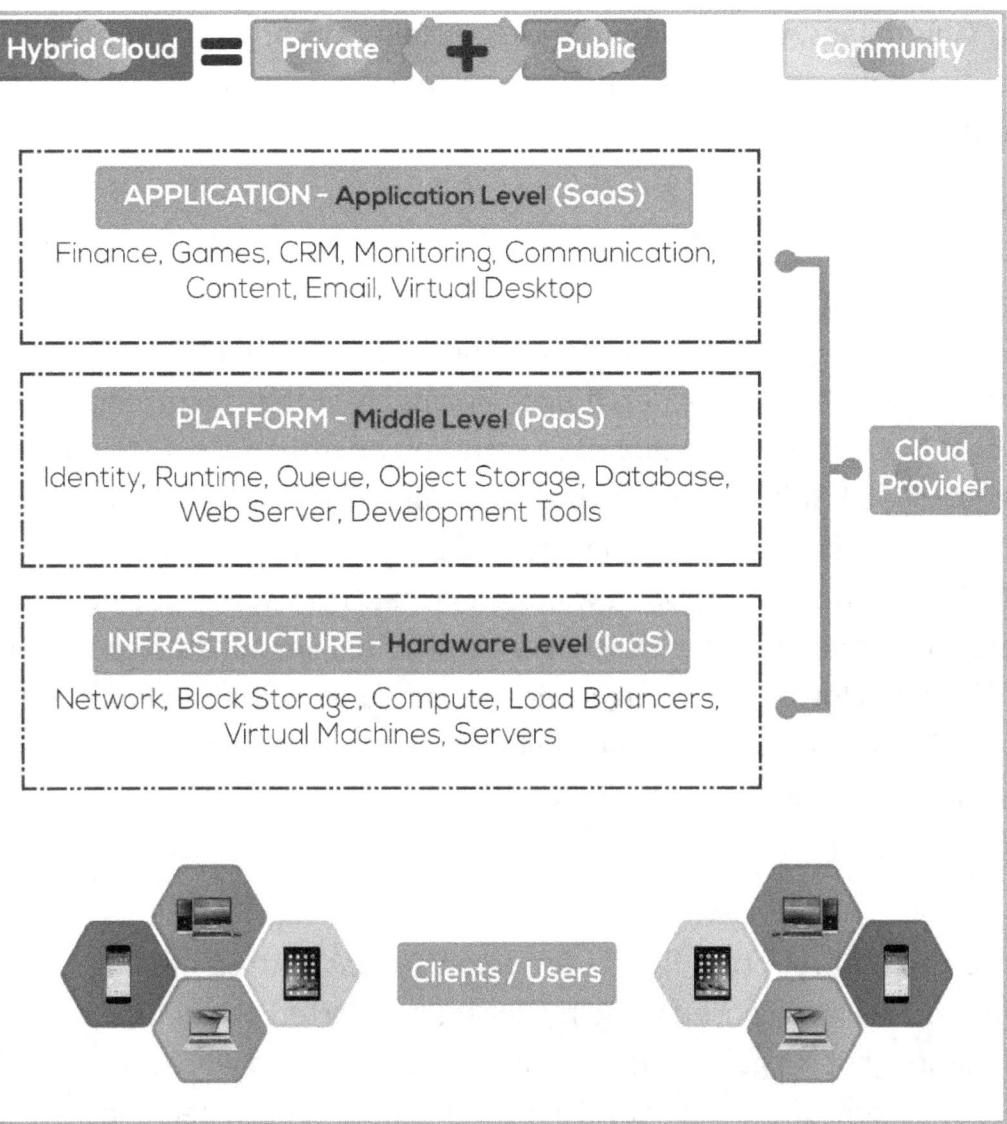

Fig. 2: Representation of the various types of cloud computing environments

Cloud Security Issues

As far back as when computers were invented, there had been IT problems due to human error. Since most machines or computers are not designed to think for themselves, they will act or deliver results based on what humans program them to do. This means, when humans make mistakes or forget to program for all eventualities, computer errors happen or systems in the cloud environment become vulnerable to malicious attacks.

Data Breaches

In 2020, the time of writing this book, there had been a trend of reports released to the public regarding companies whose data had been breached. Based on research on data breaches, it became apparent that occurrences had increased by around 80% with financial devastation on affected organisations of approximately $5.5 trillion globally, over a couple of years. The outcome of the research revealed that most of the affected organisations' problems centred on cloud misconfiguration. It was stated that this issue impacted a high percentage of organisations which had been in business or started before the year 2010, but a lower percentage were impacted of those that launched from the year 2015. That is, older companies are being impacted more than newer or younger companies (Greg, 2020).

Impacts of Cloud Misconfiguration

Evidence showed that reported figures for organisations with cloud misconfiguration were supposed to be higher than reported at the time suggested. Although it is against the law, some data breaches were left unreported. The irony of the matter is that when a data breach becomes public, more often than not, it is not the cloud provider whose image or reputation gets ruined but the organisation with the responsibility to protect customer data.

Here are the reasons why cloud misconfiguration is happening in these organisations (Greg, 2019);

- When companies are moving their systems over to the cloud
- Users with limited knowledge or a lack of IT experience

- Failing to configure assets, leaving them vulnerable to attacks
- Lack of clear cloud visibility
- Failing to change from outdated security models
- Lack of adequate cloud architecture and approach
- Unexpected rate of change, scale and scope
- Increase in attack surfaces due to the surge in cloud user number
- When undergoing mergers and acquisitions with other organisations

It is impossible to completely eradicate human error. Which means, the risks posed by these errors will continue to occur. However, something could be done to reduce the level of occurrence and save organisations money and protect their reputation. A professional and practical way to achieve this is by ensuring adequate security policies are developed but not forgetting to introduce a strategy or tool to manage them accordingly.

Data Security Strategies

One practical thing to consider is auditing (internal or external). This would enable an enterprise or organisation to develop an understanding of the type of data they possess, what part of it is valuable, and to be able to prioritise it accordingly, in terms of protection. For example, audits will enable enterprises to identify the data that is covered by security standards. Like data associated with privacy law or GDPR (Lock, 2019).

In order to help enterprises further reduce their level of cloud access risk, the adoption of the principle of least privilege should be introduced. This will mandate users to only access data, assets and resources as required to function in their role (Lock, 2019).

Organisations or enterprises are able to maintain the security of their data by introducing a central tool that would manage the activities surrounding the sensitive data. The tool will be able to monitor data access 24/7 and would be able to produce reports on when and by whom data was accessed (Lock, 2019).

Just as the internet has changed our lives all around the world in a positive way, serious problems like hacking and other social media issues have been introduced to our lives. Some of these problems are magnified in the cloud environment because it impacts on most resources and users at once.

In a multi-tenant or public cloud environment, whenever there is internet connection failure, it leads to expensive downtime for businesses that are using the cloud platform.

Similarly, when there is a slow internet connection, cloud users notice that it becomes difficult and time-consuming to access or send information. This problem is seen by cloud providers as an issue which is out of their control, except during scheduled maintenance downtime. For this reason, cloud providers are unlikely to include a clause that internet downtime will be prevented as part of their service level agreement in any contract with customers.

Chapter Three
Internet of Things (IoT)

> … Privacy and security are important areas in IoT, where the devices used are not registered, or where there is a policy for the allocation of devices to authorised people. …

The IoT in reality is a series of interconnected small devices with limited or reduced processing and storage capabilities. These devices are faced with challenges like privacy, reliability, performance, identity management and security.

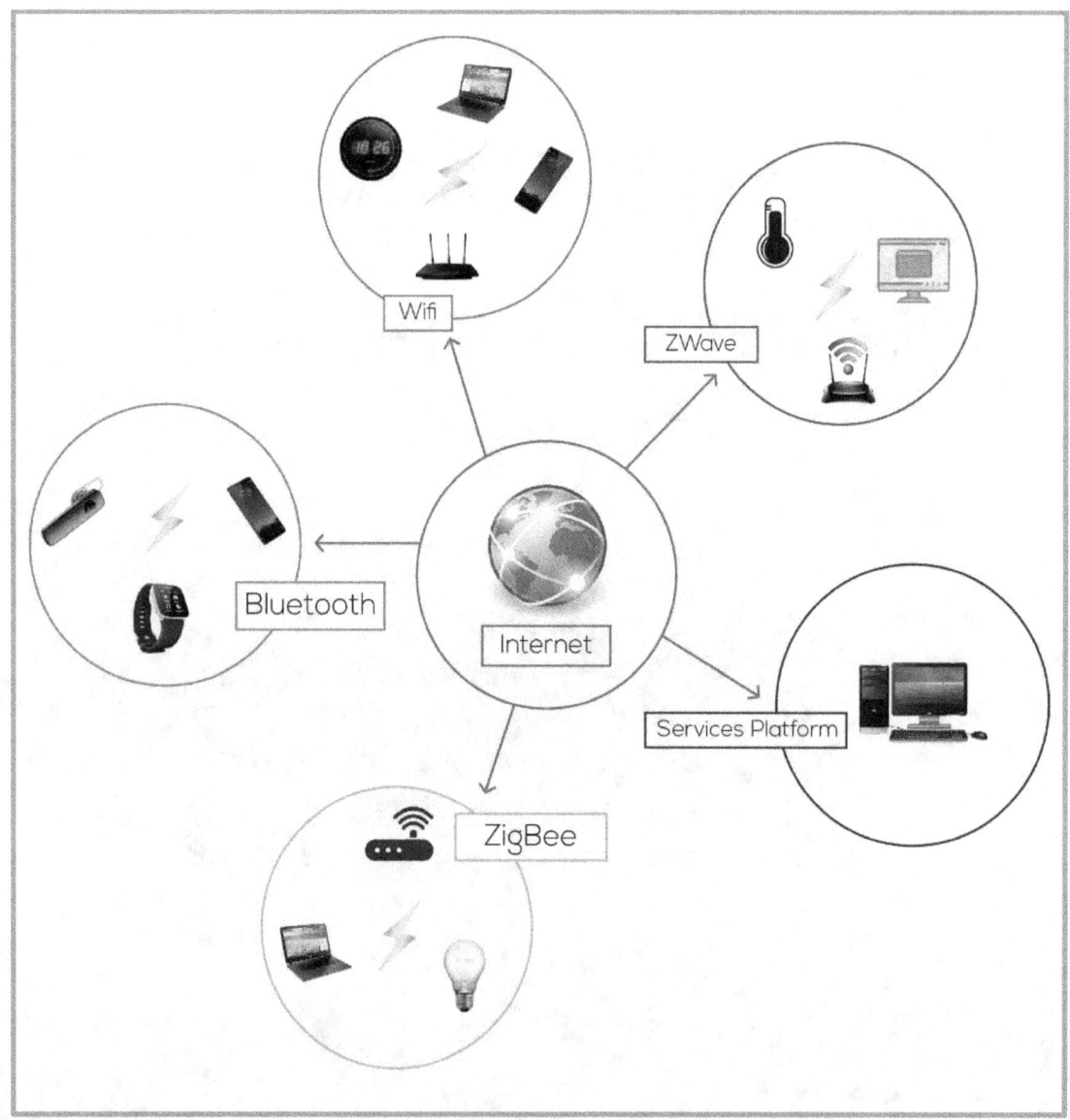

Fig. 3.1: Sample IoT connections via internet

5 Areas of IoT

The components and architectural framework of IoT can be categorised into five areas;

Perception

This area is represented by sensory components such as the Radio Frequency Identification (RFID), which acts as an electronic barcode and readily collects information.

Network

This area encompasses wireless components like Wi-Fi, Bluetooth, Infrared and others. The main function is to ensure that collected information by the perception area is transferred or correctly routed to the following areas.

Middleware

This area's main function is service management. It is able to store received data, process the data, and based on the outcome of the processing, decide on the next action.

Application

The main function of this area relates to application management, which is achieved based on the actions derived in the middleware. Applications in the present day are in the form of smart appliances. For example, smart cities, cars, homes, even fridges.

Business

The main function in this area is to analyse the information provided from the lower areas by using various analysis techniques or technologies. The output of which provides results for the business or consumer in the form of reports or graphs via a graphical interface (Sivakumar, Anuratha, Gunasekaran, 2017).

IoT Benefits

Sharing Medical Data

Internet of Things has improved the medical world in the way treatment and care is being provided. Whereas before, it was close to impossible for medical data to be shared, it is now made easy, which supports medical organisations to deliver health care effectively. They are able to do this by capturing and sharing health data between care environments and patients regardless of the differences in systems or devices used. For example, long-term ill patients can now stay at home. Instead of being admitted to hospital, they would be monitored using remote patient monitoring devices until such a time when it becomes necessary to bring them into the hospital environment.

Team Collaboration

IoT makes it possible for teams in most organisations to work together and to share information without being at the same location.

Cost Savings

In the past or in any environment where IoT devices are not in use, like a medical centre, for example, it would be a tedious process to gather medical information, monitor diagnosed illness and almost impossible to access patient records when not in a designated environment. However, with IoT, the cost associated with carrying out these activities is reduced due to the flexibility and capability of accessing patient data when required.

Predictive Maintenance

In the engineering sector, for instance, things like knowing when to ground old aircrafts and the best time to replace some faulty parts will be known well in advance by using IoT devices to monitor vital parts of the aircraft.

Supply Chain Management

In terms of real-time monitoring of equipment performance or operations at stipulated times, IoT devices would determine when different materials are produced in order to achieve making the final products. Furthermore, it could improve efficiency by determining the quantity of raw materials to procure and stock. (Spall, Marini, 2020)

IoT Disadvantages

Internet Connectivity

Like the name states, IoT is gravely dependent on a reliable internet connection. Hence, in any environment where there is limited or no internet connection possible, this will hinder the workings of devices to communicate as required. It should be said, however, that there are some organisations who have developed systems or mobile databases (e.g. NoSQL database), which may help with data processing where there is no connectivity by using mobile technology. For example, in a situation where a patient is being treated locally and there is no internet connection, the data gathered will only be held on the medical device used, until the medical practitioner returns to base before the information in the device is synced with the hospital patient's record.

Limited Storage

Most IoT devices have limited storage facility to ensure adequate processing levels. For example, when you consider the volumes of video recordings that are captured by an average security camera within 24 hrs. It hasn't got the required memory size that is big enough to store those video recordings. Hence, the data has to be transmitted and stored using a dedicated storage facility or cloud environment, which has adequate storage and processing facilities.

Data Privacy & Security

Privacy and security are important areas in IoT, where the devices used are not registered, or where there is a policy for the allocation of devices to authorised people. In such cases, the data captured by these devices can easily fall in the wrong hands. Depending on where an IoT device is being used, there is no guarantee that the network through which the captured data is transferred is secure. Hackers will be able to hack into vulnerable networks largely unseen and unheard like a ghost.

Barriers Preventing IoT Adoption

According to a report produced by the institute of mechanical engineers on "internet of things revolution 2020", based on the survey carried out over 1800 engineers globally, mixed feedback was received.

Some engineers stated that their most significant deployment concerns were put down to security and budget issues, while overall the global feedback stated their concern, centred on security and cost of IoT installations.

The security concerns were mainly about the transmission of sensitive data over the internet and the high probability of things going wrong, which would have a severe impact on safety.

They also mentioned the lack of knowledge of how the IoT devices are either applied or rolled out. In other words, there is a knowledge gap in this sector, in terms of "what IoT is" and "what IoT can do". This apparently leads to the concern about whether they are nice things to have or a must-have thing. (Spall, Marini, 2020).

In the same survey it was highlighted that as high as 85% of respondents confirmed that although they've already accepted IOT, their main concern is the fact that IoT may increase their cyber security risks. (Spall, Marini, 2020).

Integrating Cloud Computing with IoT

It is a well-established fact that IoT continues to spread into all areas of our communities. As new technologies come on the market, new and improved devices are developed. However, the capabilities and efficiencies of most of these IoT devices are limited. Hence, the idea of integrating IoT devices with cloud technology. The processing power, storage, data analytics, etc. are all limited in any IoT device but are unlimited in cloud environment. As such, an IoT device is able to generate as much data as possible, and the data, when transmitted to the cloud, is stored and processed limitlessly.

Figure 3 (below) presents the integration of cloud and IOT architectural framework nicely.
At the forefront, you have the collection of sensors and actuators with the capability to convert real-world information collected into data for analysis. This is also known as the perception part of the framework.
Then there are the data acquisition systems like WiFi, which has the capability to connect to the sensors as well as to the internet gateways, in order to continue data processing. This part ensures that data is digitised and aggregated, which makes up the network area.
A vast volume of digital data will be transmitted via the internet to designated cloud environments for analysis and processing. This part is considered the middleware. If the sensors and actuators are registered and configured then the processing done in the cloud could provide reports on analysed data from any particular device.
These processed and analysed data reports and statistical information could be presented to the users via user interfaces and applications within the business part of the framework. End users can use various types of computer applications to access the analysed data in the cloud and produce their required reporting. This would determine if the information that is collected from the front part is doing the required job or do they need some adjusting to improve data quality.

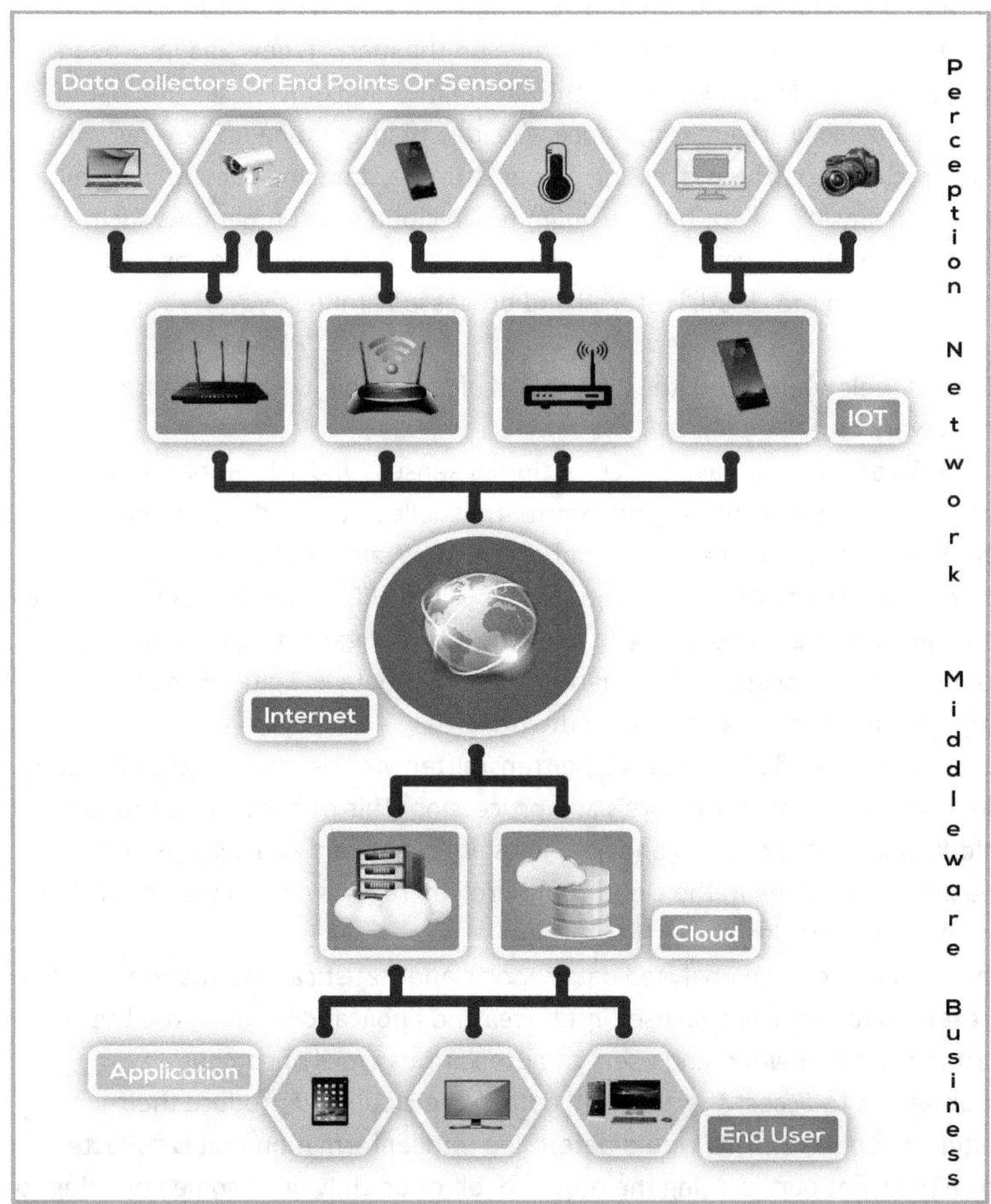

Fig. 3: The integration of cloud environment and IoT components (Sivakumar et al., 2017)

How IoT is Complemented by Cloud Computing

IoT and Cloud Computing work well when integrated. This means they compensate each other very well in many ways, thus neutralising each other's weaknesses when properly configured, as described under the following subsections below.

Storage capabilities

IoT is regarded as the source of information. As such, large varieties of unstructured data are produced. The downside is that storage space can be occupied by volumes of unstructured data. The generated data may also require a specific type of storage facility. The cloud environment will be able to provide that special storage facility and sufficient capacity, as well as determine how data is stored.

Communication capabilities

It can be costly to support IoT internet protocol enabled communication devices. However, cloud computing offers less expensive methods of connecting with many devices at any level by using well-developed apps and portals with low power data communication. There are potential communication 'bottlenecks' in situations where communication facilities are on the peripherals of internet connectivity. The reason being, large volumes of data are to be transferred to the cloud, but there is not sufficient connection to cope with the high volumes of data transfer.

In a situation where the IoT produces large volumes of data without the required processing capability, things will go wrong very quickly. The data generation could either be stopped at intervals or reduced considerably which might lead to an increase in error, cost and mistrust. However, with the cloud's unlimited processing capability, there is no need to alter the generation or flow of data.

Data Security

As mentioned above, whenever you have communication issues due to reduced or poor internet connections, it is likely to have data leakage and security issues. Unauthorised data access or data manipulation would potentially be happening. In other words, data integrity would be an issue and data captured at such location cannot be trusted.

Data Privacy

Pivacy diminishes as data or information is picked up by any IoT device and reduces further as the number of interconnected devices increases. In order to help improve the privacy of collected data, encryption during transit and on storage becomes necessary.

In a situation where you have interconnected IoT devices that are properly configured and compatible, with a good internet connection to a cloud environment, data privacy will improve significantly.

Interoperability

Due to the disparity in the devices produced or developed using different technological methods, IoT devices may sometimes not integrate well. This problem will affect IoT's ability to work efficiently as expected. By integrating cloud computing, abundant resources and developed apps are made readily available to ensure device flexibility.

Energy Consumption

The more data collected by an IoT device, the more processing power and thus energy required. Manufacturers work to shrink the processing and battery technology, but there are limits to what can be achieved. Consequently, the cloud environment uses decentralised energy to operate. Data farms can be readily constructed in new locations to handle increased IoT device data collection.

Resource allocation

As the number of IoT devices increases, it becomes a complex activity to allocate computing resources without delay. The cloud environment has a vast number of applications, resources and processing power with the capability to seamlessly identify the required resources for any connected IoT device. For example, several security cameras at various locations would be handled adequately by a dedicated cloud environment without much problem.

Identity and Access management

Due to the continuous increase in the number of IOT devices being manufactured, identifying owners and assigning appropriate access becomes more difficult indeed. However, with the presence of the cloud environment, IoT devices within a given location can be configured in order to identify each one and access privileges could also be maintained using the cloud facilities. For example, at any given time, reports could potentially be generated to show the data collected from a particular IoT device and who has access to those devices.

Chapter Four
5th Generation Networks (5G)

> ... 5G networks must improve QoS. Especially, in relation to the millimetre wave frequency, where many base stations will be deployed in close proximity ...

At the time of writing this book, the global 5G network was in early release with huge expectations for businesses and personal use. The 3GPP international project partnership decided that the 5G network standard will be known as the 5G New Radio or NR for short. The 3GPP enabled the network to accommodate a wide variety of frequencies, some of which were recycled decommissioned networks.

As network providers proceeded to develop and launch their own networks, a new generation of mobile devices was required. The 5G network is not backward compatible with existing telecom networks, all old mobile handsets couldn't be enhanced to enable 5G connectivity. The network is expected to revolutionise telecom, businesses, technology, transport, health and residential sectors among others. The 3G and 4G networks of the past provided limited wireless connectivity, whilst 5G is expected to provide businesses and consumers with limitless connectivity.

One of the most frequently asked questions is "What is different about 5G?. Simply, 5G technology or network is purpose-built for homes and businesses. Unlike previous networks, with small device group support via Wi-Fi. With 5G you are able to run a business independently without relying on any cable or wired broadband connection.

This is the fifth generation network standard, to evolve from 3G network and 4G LTE. This would establish technologies (like **network slicing** and **service function chaining**), new opportunities in bandwidth and low latency that will boost next-generation apps and tools.
Apparently, traditional network was built on capacity, but with the advent of virtualisation it would be possible to base the network build on something different. Hence, the introduction of network slicing which will take effect.

Brief History of Telecommunication

Telecommunication technology has continued to evolve every decade from the 1980s by increasing bandwidth and introducing new features. The evolutions were marked with Generations. Each of the network generations made a difference in the business world and the way we all communicate with one another. Over the period, mobile handsets of varying sizes and features emerged, followed shortly by stages of obsolescence. Handsets eventually became smaller, lighter in weight, and more densely packed with computing power and memory. The table below gives some characteristics of the global network evolution over time.

Network	Characteristics	Time Launched
Analogue	Voice calls only	1980
2G	GSM - Voice calls and Texts (SMS)	1990
2.5G	GPRS & EDGE – Packet-Switching (internet connection)	1990+
3G	UMTS - Data offering at 1Mbps	2000
3.5G	HSPA & HSPA+ - Data offering at 2Mbps	2000+
4G	LTE – Data offering at 100Mbps	2010
4.5G	LTE Advance & Advance pro – Data offering at 1Gbps	2012
5G	IMT- 2020 – Data offering at 20Gbps	2015

Table 4a: Historic information about the telecom networks over the decades (Sanders, 2018)

Consumers' and business' data demands have increased with the continual improvement in quality of service. Which has led to 5G's development being widely embraced. Consequently, the expectations on 5G were to deliver high volume connectivity to devices, with applications that could handle high data rate communication, using advanced reliability and ultra-low latency frequencies (Sanders, 2018).

What Makes a Network 5G?

A network meets the 5G classification, if the download and upload data speed are 20 and 10 Gbps respectively, as a minimum. Unlike the 4G network, with download and upload data speeds of 150 and 15 Mbps respectively (CLOUDTECH, 2019).

5G Early Development Rollouts

Given the high expectations placed on 5G, network providers all over the world took their time to schedule trial rollouts within selected cities or areas. As the technology was perfected and the required functionalities achieved, further rollouts were to be scheduled. This enabled the steady development of new applications and devices to connect the 5G network to different communities. Table 4b (below) highlights some of the rollouts in some selected countries. At the time of writing this book, Huawei is banned from deploying their 5G network in the United States and the UK, due to national security reasons. Also, Huawei and ZTE, that were both Chinese network operators, were banned from deploying their 5G network in Australia for the same reason. The concern was the possibility that Huawei would pass intellectual properties of the countries where they operate, over to the Chinese government.

Country	Network Providers	Work done	Period
Australia	Optus	5G NR deployment	2019
Australia	Telstra	5G NR deployment	2018
Barcelona	Huawei and Intel	Mobile World Congress - 5G interoperability tests	2018
Estonia	Intel, Ericsson	Connection of Tallink cruise ships to the port of Tallinn	2018
South Korea	KT, Samsung, Intel	Winter Olympics – 5G SIG - Live stream video with gigabit-speed and low latency BB	2018
Tokyo	Intel, NTT Docomo	Tokyo Olympics – 5G - 360 degree, 8K video	2020

Country	Network Providers	Work done	Period
		streaming, drones, facial recognition.	
UK	EE	5G NR deployment to 16 cities	2019
UK	Vodafone	5G NR deployment	2019
UK	Telefonica	5G NR deployment	2019
UK	Hutchinson	5G NR deployment	2019
US	Verizon	5G TF - deployment	2018
US	AT&T	5G NR deployment	2018
US	AT&T	5G NR deployment	2019
US	Sprint	5G deployment	2018
US	T-Mobile	5G NR deployment to 30 cities	2018

Table 4b: Telecom providers across selected countries and their 5G rollouts

It should be noted that 5G NR is the bandwidth that telecom providers aim to achieve, but the initial trials were based on other upgraded versions of 4G LTE. For example, you have versions such as 5G TF and 5G SIG which were deployed by Verizon and KT respectively within the period of transitioning to 5G NR.

The 5G network is made up of two different frequencies. They are FR1 (450 MHz to 6 GHz) and FR2 (24 GHz to 52 GHz). FR2 is also known as Extremely High Frequency (EHF) or millimetre wave (mmWave) (Sanders, 2018).

5G Services

It was established by the 3GPP international project partners that the 5G NR network would be able to perform successfully at a level expected because the network paradigm can create a mixture of three different services or classes which are combined in the one infrastructure. Each one makes use of the bandwidth, latency and intelligence in different ways. Such that the network provider could provide varying services by using the method of network slicing (i.e. combining multiple virtual networks with different parameters, in order to provide a service. **See Network Slicing** definition in Appendix B)

Table 4c (below) highlights the prospects of the mobile use cases based on the capabilities of the three different types of 5G services.

Service	Acronym	Benefit
Enhanced Mobile Broadband	eMBB	Provides high-level bandwidth, improves upload and download speed, provides low latency, supports and improves media applications. For example, 3D video streaming, AR and VR.
Ultra-Reliable Low-Latency Communication	uRLLC	Main focus applicable to extremely latency-sensitive or mission-critical use cases. For example, autonomous vehicles, robot-enabled remote surgery and factory automation.
Massive Machine-Type Communications	mMTC	As a narrowband access type which would be applicable for monitoring, metering and sensing use cases. For example machine to machine type communication.

Table 4c: 5G three heterogeneous classes (ITU, 2015)

Fixed-Wireless Access (FWA)

Aside from the three 5G heterogeneous services, there is another service known as the 5G fixed-wireless access or 5G-FWA.

It is a known fact that at the release of any of the telecom generation technologies (e.g. 3g or 4G), there have been collective efforts by the telecom and technology communities to substitute the use of fibre or fixed-wired cables with fixed-wireless access. However, there hasn't been a viable option until now, due to the arrival of 5G.

If you consider UK households, for example, there are rising requirements for speed and data. In order to deliver a viable solution to meet these increasing demands as quickly as possible, associated costs and the time (in terms of speed of deployment) are significant.

The fixed-wired cables are expensive (due to laying of the cables) and take time to complete the installation. However, for the fixed-wireless access or 5G-FWA, it is cheaper and could be set up in a very short time. Also, it eliminates the current method of having customers tied to long term contracts. Currently, the speed delivered by fixed-wired cables to households is averaging around 46Mbps. However, it is envisaged that the 5G-FWA will deliver on average 100Mbps but could potentially go up to 3Gbps, based on commercial trial performed with limited customer numbers (Talmesio, 2018). Which means, any area where low data speed is experienced, could benefit from the use of 5G-FWA.

The deployment of 5G-FWA means that the fixed-wireless access will benefit from key 5G technology characteristics like speed of delivery, data security and customers' quality of experience.

5G Attributes

There are some important attributes which 5G must have to enable it to meet consumer and business expectations.

Handover Process

The handover process must work seamlessly between 5G and Wi-Fi connections or drop back to 4G LTE in low coverage areas.

Quality of Service

5G networks must improve QoS. Especially in relation to the millimetre wave frequency, where many base stations will be deployed in close proximity. Within each base station, it is expected that data will be cached in order to prevent delay when data is being transmitted during video streaming for instance.

Signal Strength

The improvement of signal strength in areas (e.g. countryside or rural areas) with weak signals by introducing multiple-hops to extend the deployed 5G network.

Deployment strategy

The 5G network launch is expected to start with a combination of use cases for eMBB and FWA as initial services. Then further network development will progress into the future, in order to provide the use cases for uRLLC and mMTC.

5G vs 4G

According to the Huawei mobile operator business group CTO, there are characteristics associated with 5G which are not present in 4G that will lead to a high level of trust.

These characteristics are:

- Increased security.
- Native encryption (Not available on 4G).
- Improved privacy protection.
- Stronger security algorithm, made up of 256-bit key length instead of 128 bit as on 4G.

When a 4G handset is switched on it signals a base station. Since the data is not well encrypted, the probability of connecting to a spoofed base station is quite high. However, in the case of 5G, the probability of the same thing happening is very low because it is more secure. Consequently, all these advantages or positive characteristics would propel economic or business growth and would improve the level of trust in digital systems.

Based on a research carried out by O2 UK, it was thought that a 5G enabled road network could save UK's economy £800 million and cut down carbon dioxide emissions by 370,000 metric tonnes per year. This could be achieved if near-real-time data is transmitted with 4k video to high spec cloud-based systems. These would maintain continuous monitoring and management of the traffic flow.

The 3 characteristics of 5G network mentioned previously could be represented using the image in figure 4. This represents what future international mobile telecommunication is expected to look like due to the benefits of 5G network.
In summary, here are examples of what each one stands for.

Enhanced Mobile Broadband
This characteristic is important because it unifies the network capacity and the increased data rates that are ever-changing due to consumer demands. Consumers don't want to connect to public Wi-Fi anymore, they are craving for lightning-fast browsing on their smartphones, possess the desire to download data 20 times faster and would like better quality video calls. (Schafer, 2019). 5G is to provide data transmission speed in Gigabits per second and ensure that activities like cloud services, augmented / virtual reality, and 3D video transmission are seamless.

Massive Machine-Type Communications
5G will provide the bandwidth and strength of transmission to ensure activities around smart devices are possible. 5G capabilities will combine with IoT to handle mission-critical applications of devices such as sensor networks, connected home, smart metering, etc.
For example, the deployment of a large number of sensors within manufacturing premises to capture the functions of the machines. This would enable their predictive maintenance and temperature controls.

Ultra-Reliable and Low Latency Communications
5G is expected to provide sufficient transmission strength to support mission-critical applications, activities around industry automation and autonomous

vehicles. Not much could be upgraded from 4G to 5G with regards to the audio communication other than clarity/reliability...

First responders will benefit from the provision of low-latency. For example, a 5G-connected ambulance can manoeuvre around the city easily due to network communication to the traffic light signals and is able to communicate with designated hospitals in real time.

5G and Smart Cities

When technologies are used in cities or urban areas anywhere in the world to improve financial, environmental, communication and social wellbeing of its citizens or residents, then they are known as smart cities (Maddox, 2019).

As 5G becomes the foundation of small-cell networks, which would power the next generation of wireless network infrastructure, combined with the proliferation of IoT that would lead to further improvement of smart cities (Maddox, 2019).

Here is a list of benefits to be expected in smart cities due to 5G;

- 5G provides the platform and capability on which to scale on at a low cost.
- Estimated approximately $160 billion savings, through reductions in energy usage, traffic congestion, and fuel costs.
- Reduction in commute times, improvement in public health safety and achievement of smart grid efficiency.
- 5G-connected street lights with video cameras and detection sensors would provide information to the public safety office for immediate response.
- Combined video and AI outputs would be relayed in microseconds for quick analysis and assessment to keep the cities safe.
- First responders will benefit from the provision of low-latency. For example, 5G-connected ambulance can manoeuvre around the city easily due to network communication to the traffic light signals and are able to communicate with designated hospitals in real time.
- Autonomous (i.e. level 5, highest level autonomy possible) or driverless vehicles become a reality in smart cities.

5G would make it possible to use AI to analyse huge volumes of data collected. The outcome would lead to using the data to automate some manual processes.

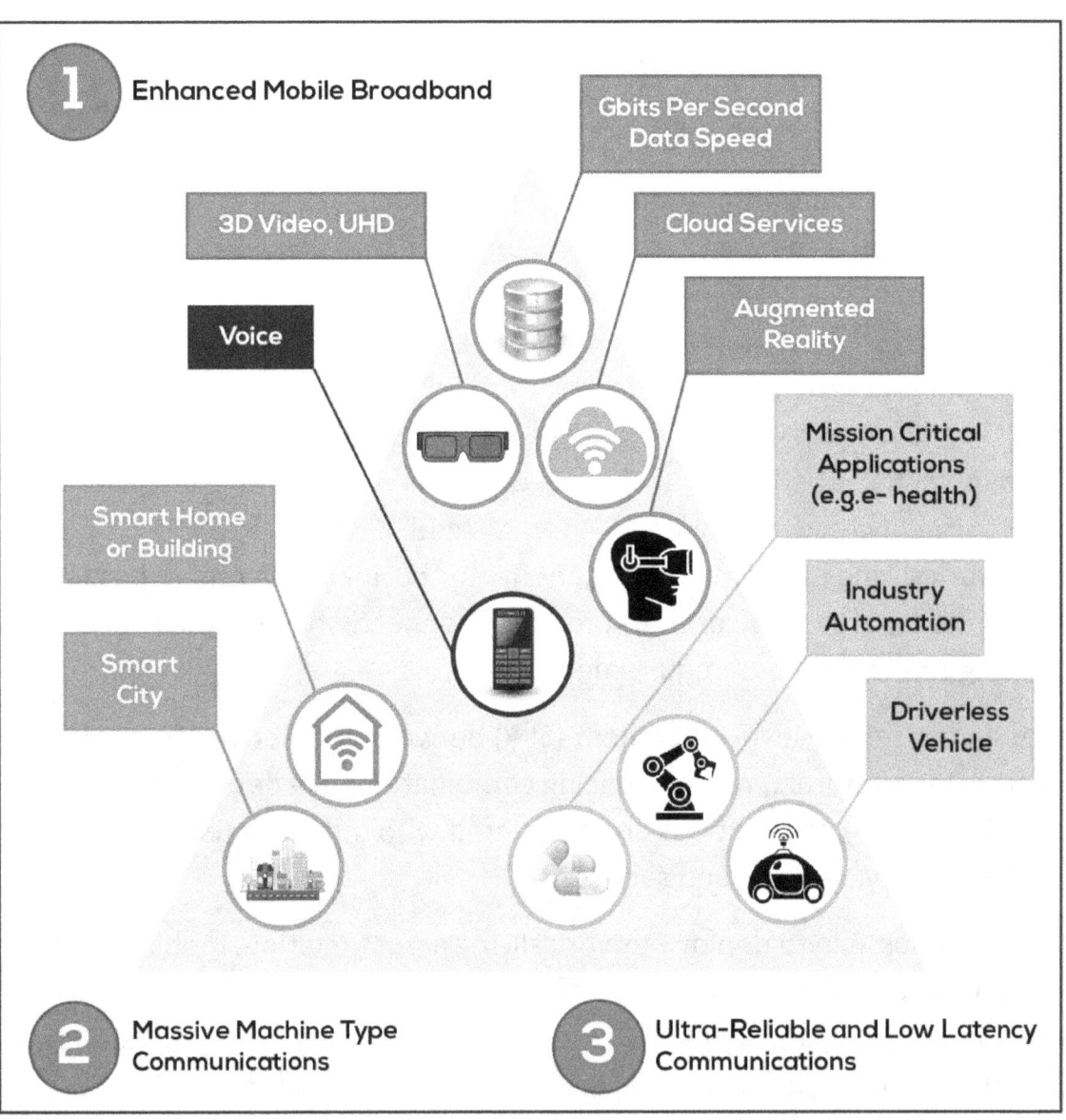

Fig.4: Future IMT for 2020 and beyond – Use cases (Sanders, 2018)

Network Slicing

Network slice could be presented as a self-contained logical network with its own virtual resources, topology, traffic flow, provisioning rules with established quality of service, security and measurable performance metrics to provide telecommunication services and network capabilities. With 5G, network slicing will come in two forms (e.g. horizontal and vertical) based on required solutions or services.

Regarding **service function chaining**, network services are able to be chained together, in order to make specific tasks a possibility. However, by combining with 5G unique qualities, this introduces different capabilities and workflows. For example, the creation of metadata updates in network slicing and also helps to simplify how network slicing is managed. (Forest, 2018).

5G network slicing has commercial benefits for business customers because it can provide tailored services (i.e. combining connectivity and data processing) according to the business' requirements.

Based on the service level agreement (SLA) between the network providers and business operators, network slicing combinations are determined. The network package combinations are associated with quality, latency, data speed, reliability, security and services.

It would be possible to deploy network slicing across multiple mobile operators and it could span across network parts like the core network, access network and transport network. Figure 4b (below) presents examples of 5G network slicing usage cases. The colours represent the slicing of different 5G bandwidths, in order to provide dedicated processing for any of the IoT activities. This would enable the network to handle more IoT activities at a given time, within a given environment, whilst maintaining an expected level of performance.

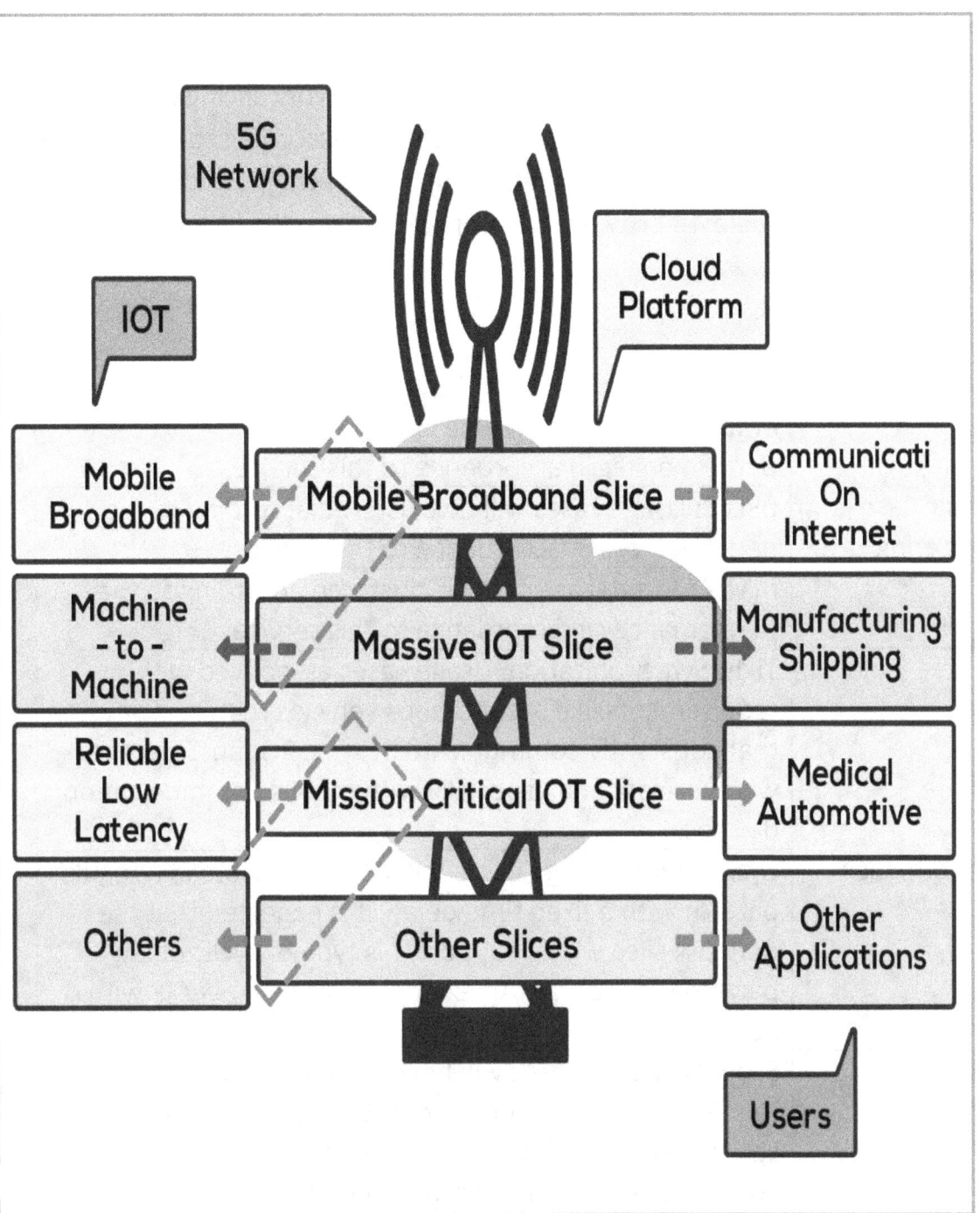

Fig. 4b: Presents 5G Network Slicing Use Cases (Mclellan, 2019)

Network Slicing Service Requirements:

This section focusses on the requirements of the network slicing model. It provides additional information on network slicing, according to the network operations. The following were still in developmental stages at the time of writing this book. Table 4d provides a list of key services and their associated requirements.

Requirement	Strategy
Usage Case Clustering	**eMBB:** Usage cases will be clustered according to their performances in accordance to this service.
	uRLLC: Usage cases will be clustered according to their performances in accordance to this service.
	mMTC: Usage cases will be clustered according to their performances in accordance to this service.
Performance	**Tight Synchronization:** Usage cases associated with requirements like autonomous vehicles require devices that constantly communicate in sync. 5G must also work with wireless and especially with mobile communication devices.
	Cyclic Traffic: Usage cases must communicate in a regular pattern with a fixed time delay. It is expected that the network slice would support this type of cyclic delay pattern without fail. An example is a voice over IP with 20 m/s inter packet delay.
Function	**Security:** Usage cases will be impacted by this requirement if or when there are security leakage. Also, security issues will vary from one use case to another. For example, communication-related to AD/VR when compared to that of health service.
	Isolation: Usage cases will need to isolate resources being shared during processing or computing activity to ensure data privacy. Customers requesting the same resources will need to be separated.
	Position Data: Usage cases might require accurate location data to enable them to perform well. This requirement will also vary according to customer activities. For example, some usage cases may work well outdoors when compared to indoors.

Requirement	Strategy
	Delay Tolerance: Usage cases will have varying levels of delay tolerance in communication. Network slicing should be able to distinguish usage cases with high communication priority and provide a lower delay latency. For example, an autonomous vehicle and application update. This requirement is expected to be part of the service level agreement in a customer contract.
	Predictive Quality of Service (QoS): Usage cases will need this to enable advanced updates to be communicated to the customer if quality of service drops below expected level. This will enable the customer to take appropriate action in advance to the QoS change. For example, changing from automatic driving to manual control in an autonomous vehicle.
Operation	**Monitoring Capability:** Must allow a network to monitor data traffic and performance characteristics. For example, the speed of data, customer location, QoS level, etc.
	Limited Control Capability: Must provide integration for customers with the use of APIs to allow flexible control without security risk.
	Configuration Capability: The customer is able to configure network function(s) provided by the network operator and also some network slice resources.
	Full Operation Capability: Customers are in full network operational control based on the capabilities provided via network slicing. Also included are the network assurance and maintenance, according to the contractual agreement with the network operator.
Coverage	**Local coverage:** This network is associated with enterprises and health centres within a geographical area. Network slice could provide this local requirement by extending the use of a VPN facility on public networks. These can be made available in small numbers of base stations in specific areas, also known as a Campus Networks. Deploying campus networks improves the speed of new hardware joining the cloud environment.

Requirement	Strategy
	Also, the coverage could be handled by a single administrative operator. **Nationwide Coverage:** This network coverage is needed by national industries within specific countries. Such as your government services, smart cities, national utilities, etc. National roaming could be deployed in a situation where there are high demand usage cases. Also, the coverage could be handled by a single administrative operator
	Global Coverage: This type of coverage is mainly for organisations or industries with a global presence. This could also be described as the roaming, transport and logistics usage cases. Network slicing would serve a customer even when the device is outside their home network. The three likely solutions are: Firstly, roaming users will have an equivalent home network slice provide by the visited network. Secondly, the blueprint of a user's network slice to be exported to the visited network in order to be configured by the visited network operator. Thirdly, the user's home network may extend the network slice into the visited network only if authorised by the visited network to be in control of the resources.

Table 4d: Network slicing requirements

5G Disadvantages:

According to a survey carried out by Tech Republic with 164 professional respondents, the disadvantage of 5G are as follows:

Lack of Availability

28% of enterprises are happy to remain on 4G network and 61% of enterprises are not ready to sign up to 5G network because of lack of availability in their area.

5G Incompatibility

57% of enterprises' perception is that their current or existing infrastructures are not compatible with 5G technology.

New Security Issues

44% of enterprises stated that their end-user is the weakest link in the security chain. Enterprises do not accept that their devices are the problem but the users of the devices. As such security training would be required both in-house and for their customers.

High Capital Expenditure

The deployment of the 5G network requires several new cell towers which comes with huge infrastructure investment costs to the service provider. At the current development stage, there is no guarantee of making any return on investment in the short term.

Lack of Backwards Compatibility

The 5G network would not work with previous-generation mobile devices. Which means, every customer would require a 5G mobile device in order to use the 5G facilities or services.

Unknown Risks with Technology in Infancy

Although the service providers understand the level of security risks that will come with the deployment of the 5G network, the issue would be whether enterprises and customers have the same level of understanding. The customers are likely to view 5G as another G model. Just like the way they handled 3G to 4G. As such, customers may not fully understand the true level of risks involved with 5G network and the need to handle it differently.

High Training Resources

When considering an enterprise's provision of IoT devices, applications, mobile devices, etc., the service provider will deploy 5G network services with the necessary changes to take care of security issues. However, enterprises or organisations must acknowledge their roles in replicating these changes to maintain the same level of security. Inevitably, there will be a knowledge gap between the service provider and the customer, which would be bridged over time, but requires early support if security risks are to be reduced.

Manufacturing Cost & Sale Price

Due to the differences in the radio modem and the antenna of the 5G from that of the 4G, it is more complicated to produce 5G smartphones when compared with 4G. As such, 5G smartphones will be more expensive to purchase.

Chapter Five
Integration of the Cloud & 5G Network

> ... Whatever the level of the cloud's processing power, 5G low latency would be capable of handling the speed of communication ...

The launch of the 5G network couldn't have come at a better time because integrating the network with IoT as there was to be an explosion of IoT enable devices due to reduced manufacturing costs. The performance of IoT devices over 4G network, for example, was limited due to speed and network coverage. Even when there are devices with improved capacity or capability, the 4G network had peaked and wasn't able to do more for the currently available IoT devices. 5G was to move IoT into a higher performance level and open new opportunities for high calibre IoT devices. No matter the volume of data generated by any IoT device, the speed of communication provided by the 5G network would be capable of handling it. This will develop smart cities, smart homes, smart health centres, driverless cars, remote surgery, traffic control, etc.

According to figure 5 below, the IoT devices located in a smart home, for instance, will transmit data collected wirelessly via a broadband or Wi-Fi through 5G network to the end-user, who is also connected to broadband at the other end.

The end-users are able to communicate with the IoT device by sending computer commands or instructions using various applications.

The gold-coloured lightening-strike signs depict wireless communications between devices like broadband and the 5G network.

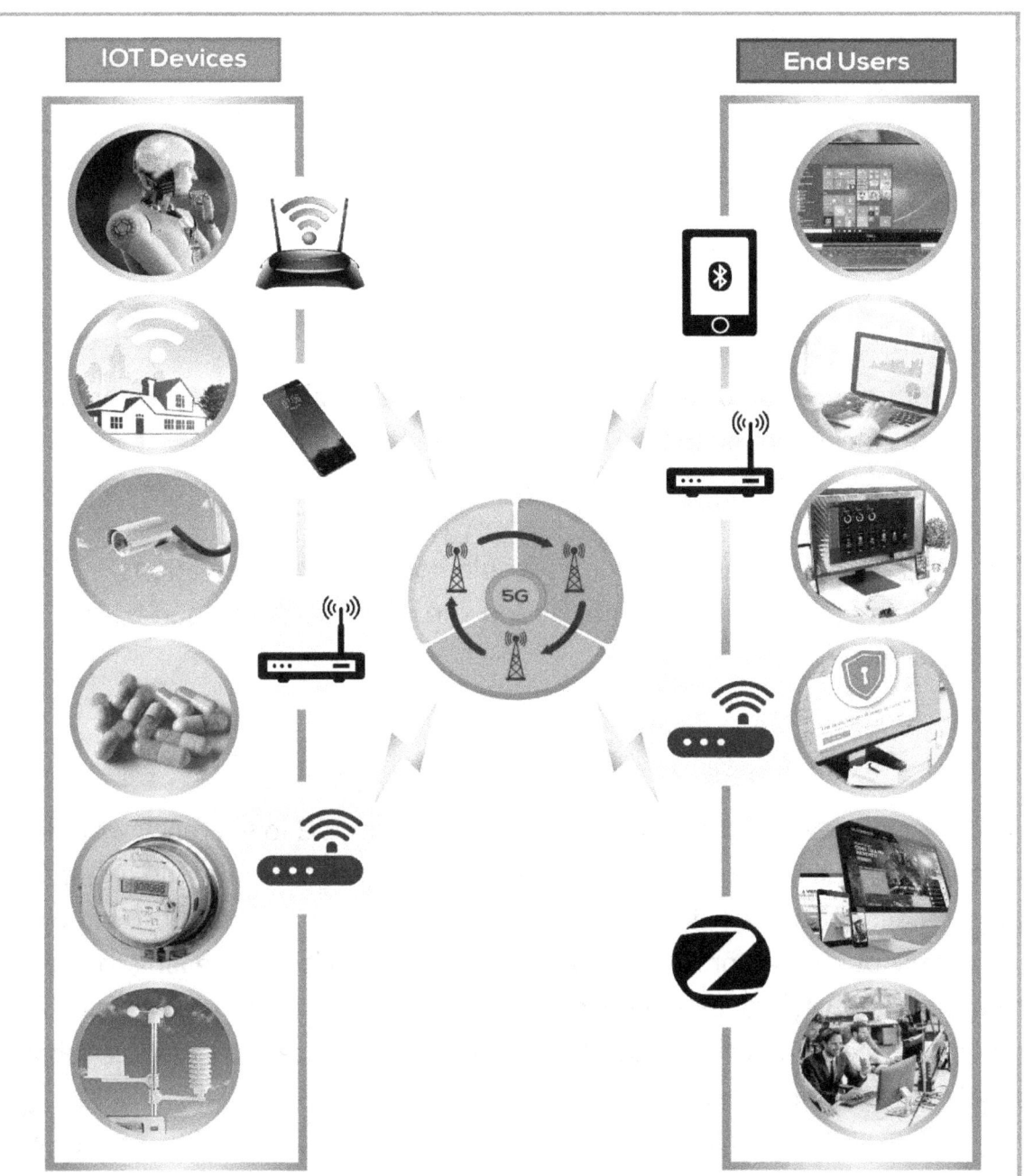

Fig. 5a: Integration of IoT and 5G technology

Integration Advantages

Bringing these two technologies together has its advantages and disadvantages. By comparison, it can be argued that the advantages outweigh the disadvantages.

Businesses and the Cloud

The rollout of 5G would significantly improve the uptake of cloud computing by businesses including those that currently have broadband.

Cloud with 5G Performance

The integration of both technologies would boost future innovations, invariably improving the reliability, speed and efficiencies of cloud-based products and services.

Processing Power & Speed

Whatever the level of the cloud's processing power, 5G low latency would be capable of handling the speed of communication. For example, the quality and speed of activities a robot or machine could perform could be improved by using the cloud's high processing power. This is especially appealing for the integration of Artificial Intelligence and Natural Language Processing for enterprises. Such that the cloud storage and real-time data transfer capability of 5G could be harnessed.

Cost Reduction

Due to the high level of processing power in the cloud, most devices will require fewer or no embedded processors.

Network and System Updates

Updates and maintenance on both technologies are completed automatically without conflict. Connected devices can maintain their own updates ensuring continual performance.

Independent Smart Devices

Smart devices with limited storage capacity are able to make use of the cloud's storage with 5G low latency. The user will avoid having to sync their smart device (like a wearable) to their smartphones before using it.

Edge Computing

The performance of mobile and remote devices on the fringes of internet connectivity is improved greatly with the 5G connection. Large data would be transferred over the 5G network to enable remote systems like location tracking Apps to work more efficiently.

Enhance Virtual Reality and Augmented Reality

Some industries like healthcare or travel would experience new innovations where VR and AR applications are greatly enhanced.

Integration Disadvantages

In a situation where a similar service could be provided using either the cloud or 5G network, depending on various factors, it is likely that one outshines the other and as such will probably be selected to deliver the service. For example, transmitting a video from one device to multiple devices is better handled by the 5G network. This would remove the delay of storing a copy of the video in the cloud, to begin with, before streaming is done. In this scenario integrating the cloud environment and 5G network will not work or not a good alternative.

According to the 3GPP release 15 standards, the 5G network associated devices are non-standalone devices. This means these devices cannot perform independently but would require alterations to meet network standards and infrastructure.

Communication between some IoT devices and the 5G network may not be guaranteed. Since IoT devices have varying types of communication interfaces, without having a standard interface, there are likely to be communication problems.

Data security will be affected where there are communication problems because hackers could use these problems to their advantage.

In a situation where endpoints or sensors of IoT devices are capturing vast volume of data in an area with limited 5G coverage, would lead to delay in data transmission and processing.

While 5G networks are still being rolled out and not fully operational in some areas, sectors like road safety (due to limited mobile coverage), transport (autonomous vehicle - unavailable low-latency capability) and health care (unable to handle some treatments remotely), will be impacted.

Chapter Six
Integration of the Cloud, IoT & 5G

> ... Some businesses will benefit more than others based on how compatible the three technologies are with their existing infrastructure and area of coverage ...

This chapter will deal with the integration of the three technologies, its security issues, advantages and disadvantages. Based on the research outcomes in the previous chapters, this chapter will bring all the information together to highlight key areas which would be useful for businesses and consumers. Additional information will also be provided in the appendices.

Some businesses will benefit more than others based on how compatible the three technologies are with their existing infrastructure and area of coverage (i.e. in terms of availability). For example, a business that requires high-speed data generation and delivery, large volumes of storage space, high levels of computing power, and millions of accessible consumers at any given time, will benefit from the integration of the three technologies.

The creation of smart cities will no longer be a dream but a reality. According to (Maddox, 2019), smart cities will depend on data gathering through huge numbers of smart devices with built-in sensors. The captured data will be analysed to determine how best to manage assets, resources and services more efficiently. Consequently, this would lead to cost savings and other benefits for businesses. Business areas like transportation, hospitals, power plants, waste management, water management, environmental issue management firms.

Figure 6 (below) provides a holistic view of an integrated sample.
The diagram is just a representation of what the connectivity of the three technologies will look like.
The IoT devices and sensors will transmit a large volume of digital data which would be transmitted wirelessly either directly to the cloud environment or via the 5G network to the end-user based on the business sector.
Attached to each type of cloud environment is the "Bridge" label. Which is the indication that the private and public clouds are connected together, in order to provide the resources needed by the hybrid cloud.
The end-users are able to wirelessly access the clouds via devices like Wi-Fi and 5G networks depending on the complexity or speed of the data involved. Previous chapters explain how the connectivity of the technologies really works.
The gold-coloured lightening-strike signs depict wireless communications between devices like broadband and the 5G network.

Security and Issues

For organisations that are migrating into the mobile cloud system, a thorough investigation has to be done in relation to improving their security architecture and security policy.

As the number of IoT devices grows, the number of security problems they will introduce increases due to factors like lack of standardisation, appraised security, lack of owners' regulation and registration, etc.

In terms of network slicing, although 5G functionality will have international roaming standards, however, the rules of how this will be used may differ as you move from one country to another. Which means, every country's legislation will impact on what network providers are able to do for their roaming customers. If current international roaming is anything to go by, there could be security issues because there is no guarantee of expected coverage as customers move from one country to another.

Due to a known security problem with cloud misconfiguration, this would lead to severe security issues where the cloud environment is linked to a 5G network. The speed at which unauthorised access of data will take place would make it almost impossible for the owners of the cloud environments to be aware that their systems had been infiltrated, unless when the intrusion leads to malicious activities.

As the 5G network rollout and uptake increases, the areas with limited coverage would impact on data security. Especially where there are likely weak signal spots, the probability of security impacts would be high during the handover from the 5G network to a lower network.

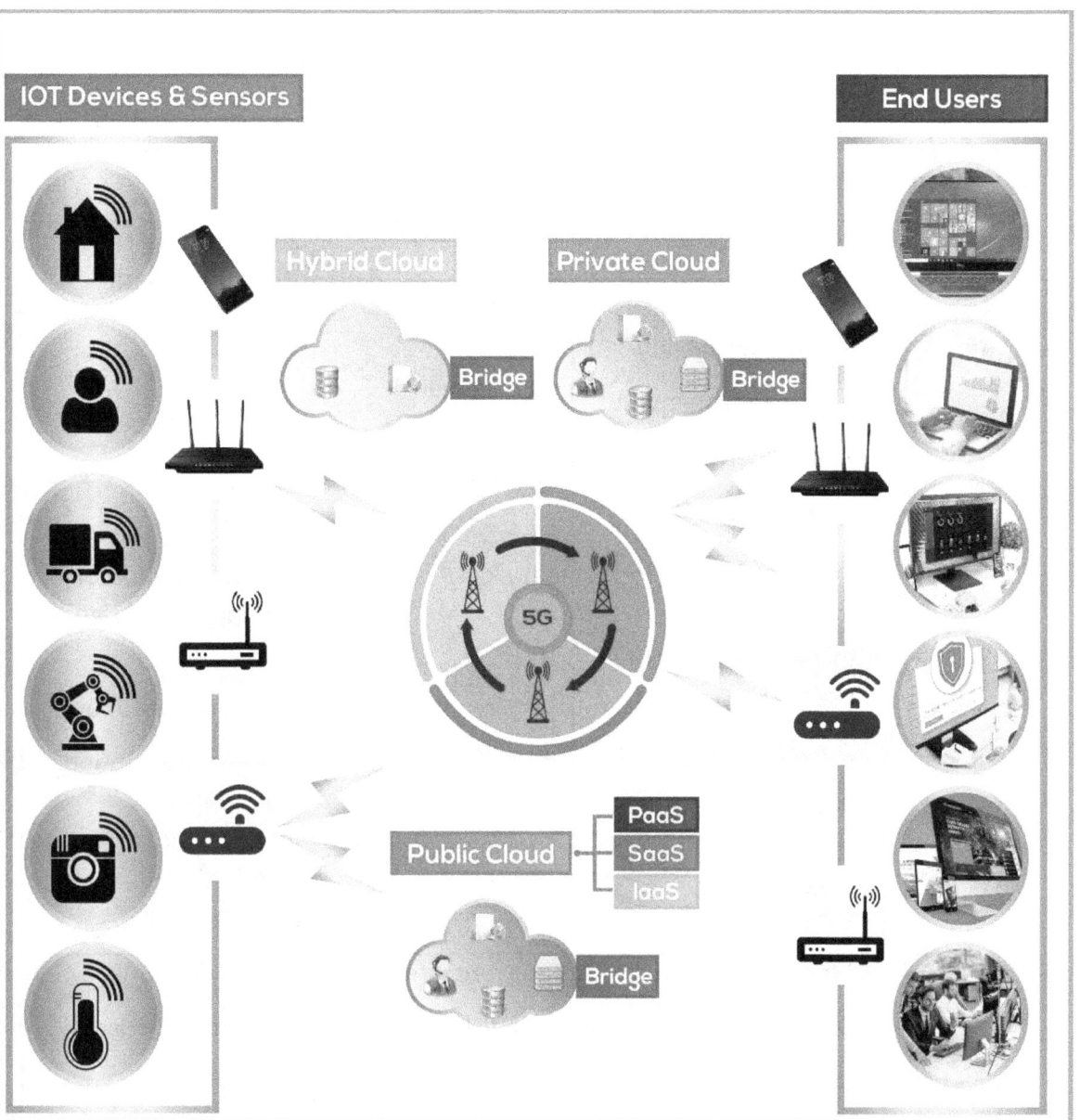

Fig. 6: Shows the integration of cloud, IoT and 5G technologies

Matrix of different factors of the technologies – Table 1

Users/Businesses	Cloud	IoT	5G
Security Requirements	Data privacy. Data security. System availability. Access management. System certification. Independent audit. Regular infrastructure maintenance. Increase in growth user risks. Security configuration. Regular internet connectivity.	Data privacy. Data security. Access management. Regular device maintenance. Remove or reduce data loss.	Zero or Low latency. High-speed data transmission. Data privacy. Data security. Security risks awareness. Maintain mandatory minimum level signal strength. Access management. Regular base stations maintenance. International roaming standards & agreements.
Security Threats	Malware infection. Data fishing. Data compromise. Lack of data privacy. Unauthorised access or hacking. Wrong or inappropriate security policies. Lack of security skills or knowledge. Security misconfiguration. Internet downtime.	Malware infection. Data fishing. Data loss. Data compromise. Unauthorised access or hacking. Wrong or inappropriate security policies. Lack of security skills or knowledge. Weak device inter-operability.	Lack of data privacy. Data compromise. Data loss. Drop-in signal strength (especially during a handover scenario). Signal interference. Inadequate or high latency. National and international weak signal spots. Rule of law conflicts between countries

Users/ Businesses	Cloud	IoT	5G
Security Solutions	Availability of Security skills and knowledge base. Regular independent audits. Intrusion detection monitoring. Regular software updates. Infrastructure upgrades. Data encryption (either in transit or in storage). Use of AI and machine learning. Cyber Insurance. Add cloud security to the list of priorities from the beginning. Maintain a dynamic and continuous secure cloud configuration process. Planned cloud maintenance to reduce systems downtime. Regular checks of the internet to avoid slow connections or failure.	Regulate the process of device connectivity. Consumer or user must be registered. Software updates must be monitored. Regression testing must be done after infrastructure or software upgrades. Cyber Insurance.	Adequate and thorough level of testing. Awareness of telecom security. Required security skills and knowledge. Regular annual network audits. Use of AI in 5G handsets or smartphones. Cyber Insurance. Replacement of slow wired internet connections with fast wireless connections. Guaranteed QoS (i.e. national & international).
Benefits	Improve and provide adequate storage facility. Provide computing power Provide services like IaaS, SaaS, PaaS, etc. Offers redundancy, stability and security	Cost savings. Data share. Remote patient monitoring. Provide standard interfaces at the point of data transfer or aggregation due to	High speed of transmission. Zero or Low latency of between 1 to 4 milliseconds approx. Improve signal strength in affected areas.

Users/ Businesses	Cloud	IoT	5G
	to users and enterprises. Eliminates the issue around purchasing and maintenance of hardware Provides remote access capabilities. Capable of scaling up or down according to business requirements. Provides both managed and unmanaged services. Cost-effective for most businesses 24/7 system availability	heterogeneous device use. For commercial businesses and manufacturing – to control robotic operations, delivers real-time analytics and provides diagnostics information. For the retail industries – tracking of inventory, online clients servicing and providing consumer analytics. For healthcare – Various Apps used for health care monitoring and safety measure for personal records.	Very high bandwidth applications on mobile. Signal handover or fall back to a lower network is seamless. Remote workers & offsite job locations. Support millions of IoT devices per square mile. Lower barriers to network connectivity for IoT devices. Network slicing will enable the provision of varying network services. Data privacy is maintained due to encryption functionality. Has high level of trust when compared to 4G network. Probability ROI is high. Serve as FWA in place of wired connections. Energy savings. High volume simultaneous device connectivity. Greater system capacity.

Table 6b-1: Presents requirements, threats, solutions and benefits of the 3 technologies

Integration of the 3 Technologies – Table 2

Users/ Businesses	Cloud / IoT / 5G
Security Requirements	Data privacy. Data security. Data Integrity. Zero or Low latency. Edge Computing Cloud storage High-speed data transmission. System availability. Access management. Regular maintenance. Regular internet connectivity. International roaming standards & agreements.
Security Threats	Malware infection. Data fishing. Data compromise. Lack of data privacy. Unauthorised access or hacking. Wrong or inappropriate security policies. Lack of security skills or knowledge. Internet connection downtime. National and international weak signal spots. Rule of law conflicts between countries.
Security Solutions	Availability of Security skills and knowledge base. Regular independent audits. Intrusion detection monitoring. Regular software updates. Infrastructure upgrades. Data encryption (either in transit or in storage). Regression and E2E testing must be done after infrastructure or software upgrades. Use of AI and machine learning. Cyber Insurance. Replacement of slow wired internet connections with fast wireless connections. Guaranteed QoS (i.e. national & international).

Users/ Businesses	Cloud / IoT / 5G
	Scalable cloud environment.
	Low latency.
	Massive connectivity.
Benefits	Provide end to end transactions.
	Enhance customer and user experience.
	creates complete smart cities &
	Smart transportation.
	Good health service.
	Creates high processing or computing power.
	Provides adequate storage facility.
	Quick resource allocation.
	Reduce procurement cost of infrastructure.
	Increase business revenue
	Provides new business opportunities.
	Data privacy is maintained due to encryption functionality.
	5G has high level of trust when compared to 4G network.
	Probability ROI is high.
	Fast internet connection.
	Controlled and elimination of internet downtime.
	Good roaming user experience.

Table 6b-2: Requirements, threats, solutions and benefits of the 3 integrated technologies

Chapter Seven

Conclusions

> ... The integration of the cloud, Internet of Things and 5G network will produce benefits for both businesses and consumers. This will also enable the evolution of things like ...

Public cloud provides flexibility in its core offerings by accessing a variety of emerging technologies required by IT organisations. This is due to the varied needs when adopting the public cloud for business. For example, IBM and VMware cloud solution.

For organisations who are either thinking of migrating their data to the cloud or already using cloud services, it is good practice to ensure cloud security is at the top of their agenda from the start. There should be continuous security checks in order to keep abreast of any system changes and avoid security issues caused by cloud misconfiguration.

It is a known fact based on surveys and known investments by some businesses that IoT has incredible potential across the engineering and many other sectors. However, the automotive sector is one of the sectors that will be significantly transformed. The adoption of IoT devices within the transportation systems has introduced visible operational changes. Most modern vehicles and electric autonomous vehicles have advanced driver-assistance systems (ADAS) fitted and some organisations will continue to invest heavily in IoT technology. (Spall, Marini, 2020).

Even with the increasing popularity of IoT technology in the transportation sector, feedback received from 47% of the 238 engineers surveyed, confirmed that safety is the most important factor for them to consider before using an IoT device. (Spall, Marini, 2020).

There has been a significant improvement brought about by the integration of cloud computing with the Internet of Things. The IoT devices and level of services provided for a potential consumer or organisation has grown. Some of the security threats associated with the IoT concept has diminished due to the secure operating software present in the cloud environment.

As innovations within the telecom industry continue, it is envisaged that older devices and networks will become obsolete. Similar to when the analogue TV signals were turned off in October 2012 and replaced with digital signals, this has already started by some telecom providers like Verizon in the United States. They scheduled to disable their 2G and 3G networks in 2019, AT&T's 2G network was disabled prior to this book's release, O2 UK planned to disable some of their 3G network. Disabling and recycling the old networks will free up the network spectrum for the 5G LTE network development.

As it has been said, the development of the 5G network will revolutionise the telecom industry as we know it, not least the reduction of the wireline broadband in areas where similar or same services are provided. It would be easier to deploy the 5G network in remote areas for instance, where broadband connections are poor. It is presumed the 5G network will enable the deployment of millions of new IoT devices in its first year or two.

By leveraging networks of IoT devices, enterprises and businesses are able to benefit from the 5G network immediately. 4G coverage is concentrated in cities and other urban centres and these suffer from device congestion.

Due to 5G network technological advancement and the huge benefits that could be harnessed, some organisations are likely to create or deploy their own 5G network. This is to improve their clients' and employees' experiences, where there would be a high difference in user experience to boost business performance and in turn boost ROI.

The integration of the cloud, Internet of Things and 5G network will produce benefits for both businesses and consumers. This will also enable the evolution of things like new devices, new businesses, intelligent applications, improved business revenue generation and possibly reduce operation costs for some businesses. However, this will introduce new or zero-day threats or security risks due to some factors which will become clearer as things develop.

In chapter one, the importance of the security risk levels of integrating the technologies was highlighted. At this stage, if we check the risk levels again based on the outcome of the research carried out, then the diagram will look like what you have below.

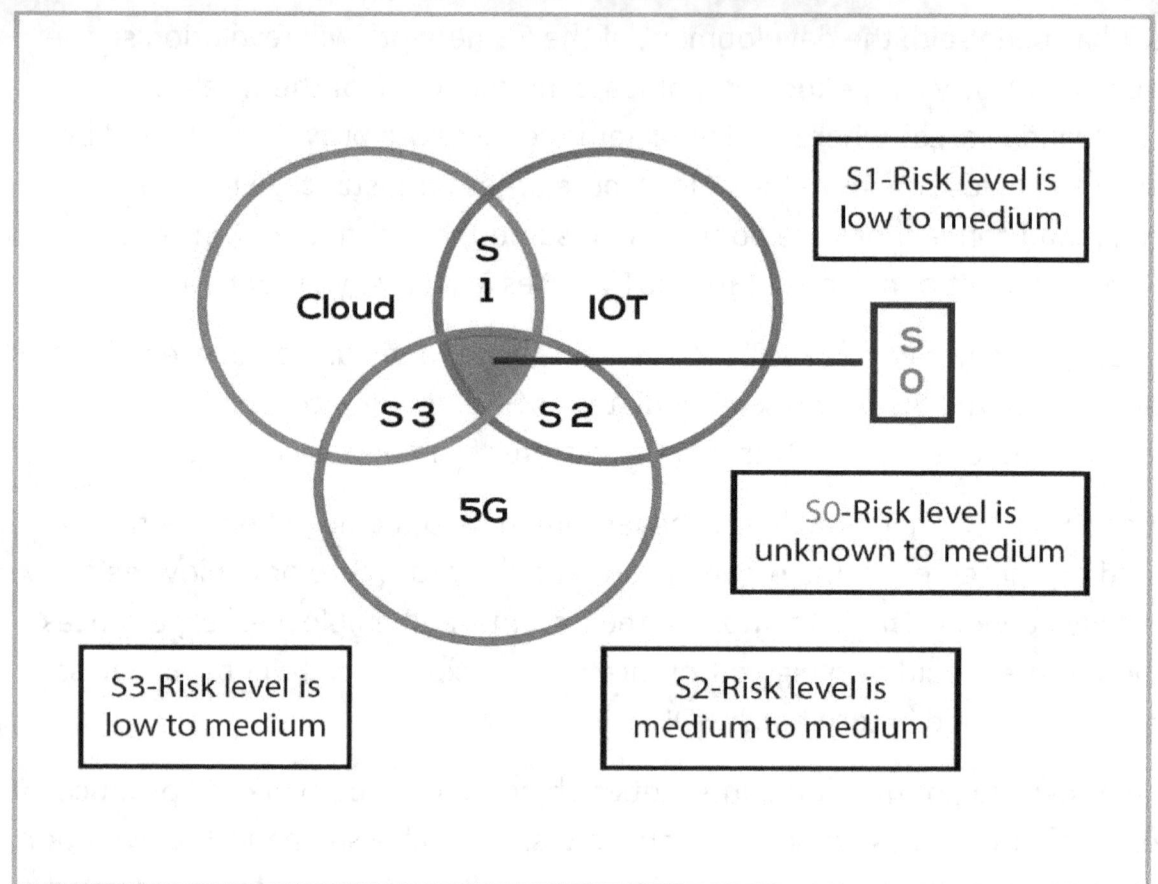

The concept of network slicing as part of providing varying services on the 5G network will benefit consumers, vertical customers and network operators. Network operators will have optimal control of the resources and will determine the level at which vertical customers will be given authorisation to control some of the resources.

Most facilities or services which would rely on the integration of cloud, IoT and 5G network technologies for their daily operations will benefit greatly. These services or devices will have the capability to enhance their functionality by pulling on the best aspects of each part of the technologies when needed. The rate at which new technologies and devices are adopted will grow exponentially within the next few years. Consequently, many devices and services which do not adhere to the technological changes will likely become obsolete.

The information in this document is not exhaustive and is expected to grow or expand over time. However, this book provides the facts as they currently are on the three different technologies and their benefits.

To help shed light on the importance of the three technologies, one must compare their growth over the past few years and the likely growth in the future. Based on the research carried out in order to write this book, there is evidence that the number of users of the cloud is on the increase for several reasons. IoT devices are also on the increase and new services are being provided. The uptake of the 5G network by organisations for different business reasons will be small initially but numbers will increase significantly over time, as most of the concerns become addressed.

Figure 7 (below) shows the growth of usage in each one of the technologies over a decade.

Whilst the fight to contain and reduce the mortality rate caused by Covid-19 goes on, lessons have to be learnt from the errors made in the beginning and also during the time the virus was spreading. The use of available technologies helped the world to maintain the operations of key facilities in many ways but did not serve everyone due to several reasons. According to the saying, necessity is the mother of invention. I believe we would be better prepared for any future attacks because, without a doubt, these three technologies will continue to evolve and would revolutionise our future in more ways than one.

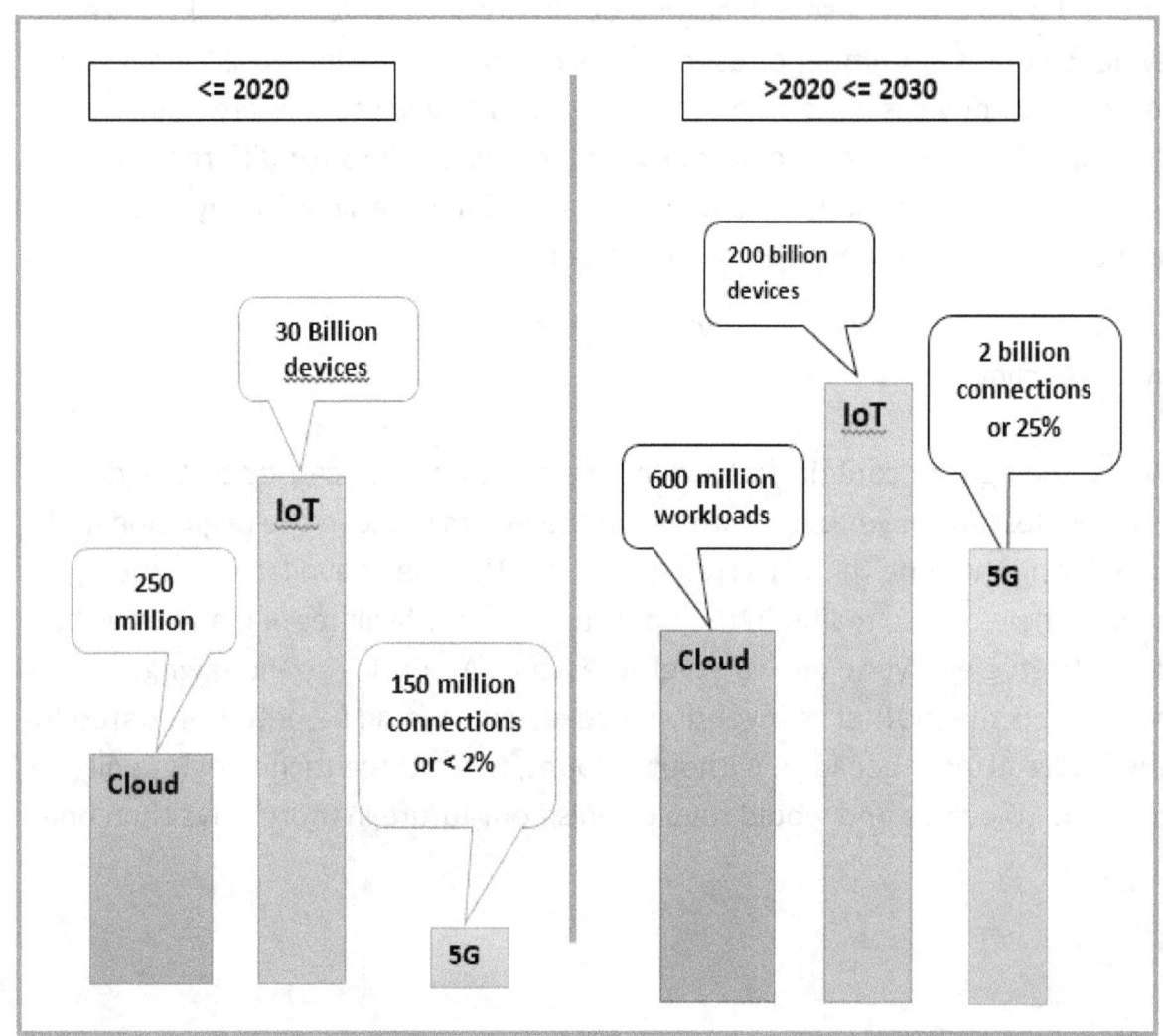

Fig. 7: Comparing the growth of usage or connections over the given period (VMWare, 2016)

Recommendations

In the digital age, businesses and enterprises have some important decisions to consider in order to achieve successful results. It would be expected for enterprises to consider their business goals and objectives, before deciding on which cloud environment is suitable for them. In the same token, it would be appropriate to ensure the correct volumes of business data are migrated to the cloud. To help arrive at an appropriate decision, an effective plan must be put in place ensuring the right questions are asked of the provider.

Based on researched information, it is clear that as new IoT devices come to market, the introduction of security issues will increase significantly. Most of the systems which are connected to these new devices would be vulnerable. Consequently, this puts the onus on businesses to perform thorough security checks or tests, before making use of any device. This is not the time for businesses to be complacent about using any device for the sake of using something on-trend, instead, they should consider the financial impact on the business or social impact on their employees.

The outcomes of researches and surveys have shown that the adoption of IoT technology varies as you go from one sector to another, mainly due to security and safety concerns. In order to improve business concerns and increase the adoption of IoT technology across most sectors, training on this technology should be introduced in every sector. This would lead to a better understanding of "what they are", "how they are used", "when they should be used", associated costs and expected ROI that will be achieved when the technology is adopted.

With 5G technology, it is apparent at this stage that not all businesses will benefit from it because of the limited coverage and due to limited 5G devices. However, with time as the coverage and number of devices improves business uptake will increase. Again, just like the suggestions given above on the cloud and IoT, regarding systems' security, the same thing applies to 5G. Even when speed is important, data and systems' security must not be ignored. The list of 5G security issues is covered in chapter six of this book.

The beauty of these three technologies is when they are integrated. Businesses would appreciate the vast options at their disposal to enable them to drive their business objectives in a preferred direction. For these integrated systems to work successfully, it would require proper planning, attention to detail, accurate configuration, skilled resources, security monitoring and adequate testing.

The future looks bright for those enterprises and individuals who are ready to take advantage of the digital evolution's benefits. Whilst at the same time be prepared to carry out the due diligence required to ensure their systems' security aspects are closely monitored and protected.

References:

Botta, A., Donato, D.W, Persico, V. and Pescap´e, A. (2015) 'Integration of cloud computing and Internet of Things: A survey, Future Generation Computer Systems' Available at: http://dx.doi.org/10.1016/j.future.2015.09.021 (Accessed: 08 December 2019)

Comparethecloud.net (2020), 'How 5G Will Accelerate Cloud Business Investment', Available at:
https://www.comparethecloud.net/articles/how-5g-will-accelerate-cloud-business-investment/, (Accessed: 10 April 2020)

Deloitte.com (2019), 'The new network arrives – TMT predictions', Available at:

https://www2.deloitte.com/us/en/insights/industry/technology/technology-media-and-telecom-predictions/5g-wireless-technology-market.html (Accessed: 10 April 2020)

Forest, C., (2018), TechRepublic.com, 'Understanding the value of network slicing and SFC in 5G wireless', 28th Aug. 2018, Available at: https://www.techrepublic.com/, (Accessed on 10th April, 2020).

Forrest, C (2016) TechRepublic.com '15 most important hybrid cloud vendors' Available at:

https://www.techrepublic.com/, (Accessed: 11th April, 2020)

Foster, B. (2019) CLOUDTECH 'Best security practices for migrating to the cloud: A guide', Available at:

https://cloudcomputing-news.net/ (Accessed: 07 November 2019)

Geller, M., Nair, P., '5g-security-innov-wp.pdf'

Greg, J. (2020) TechRepublic.com '5G expansion continues but devices struggle to keep up', Jan. 2020, Available at:

https://www.techrepublic.com/meet-the-team/us/jonathan-greig/, (Accessed: 10 April 2020)

Greig, J. (2020), TechRepublic.com, 'Security, Cloud misconfiguration', Available at:

https://www.techrepublic.com/topic/security/ (Access: 14 April 2020)

GSMA.com (2018), 'An introduction to network slicing', PP. 3-59, Available at:
https://www.gsma.com/futurenetworks/, (Accessed: 07 December 2019)

Integration of Cloud computing and Internet of Things: A survey – FGCS cloudIOt15.pdf

Investopedia.com (2019), 'Cloud Computing', 18th May, 2019, Available at: https://www.investopedia.com/terms/c/cloud-computing.asp, (Accessed: 3rd July, 2020)

ITU (2015), 'IMT Vision – Framework and overall objectives of the future development of IMT for 2020 and beyond', Sept. 2015, Available at: http://www.itu.int/ITU-R/go/patents/en, (Accessed: 07 December 2019)

Jackson, C. (2017), Quest Software Inc. 'Moving your databases to the cloud', PP. 2-21, Available at: https://www.quest.com/whitepaper/moving-your-databases-to-the-cloud8129717/ (Accessed; 05 October 2019)

Lia, S., Xub, L. D. and Zhaoe, S. (2017), '5G Internet of Things: A Survey', Research Repository, 16th December 2017, Available at: https://uwe-repository.worktribe.com/output/871346/5g-internet-of-things-a-survey, (Accessed: 10 October 2019)

Lin, B.-S. P., Lin, F. J. and Tung, L. –P. (2016) 'The Roles of 5G Mobile Broadband in the development of IoT, Big Data, Cloud and SDN', Communications and Network, 8, 9-21 Feb. 2016, Available at: https://www.scirp.org/journal/paperinformation.aspx?paperid=63807, (Accessed: 11 April 2020)

Linthicum, D. (2018), InfoWorld.com, '5G will bring cloud computing to everyone' Available at: https://www.infoworld.com/article/3308378/5g-will-bring-cloud-computing-to-everyone.html, 25th Sept. 2018, (Accessed: 10 April 2020)

Linthicum, D. (2018) Infoworld.com 'Cloud Computing', 25th Sept. 2018, Available at: https://www.infoworld.com/article/3308378/5g-will-bring-cloud-computing-to-everyone.html, (Accessed: 12 April 2020)

Lock, M. (2019) CLOUDTECH 'Eradicate human error and make your cloud implementation a picnic' Available: https://cloudcomputing-news.net/news/?user=25516 (Accessed: 10 October 2019)

Maritz, P. (YR) 'Eye opening facts about cloud computing', VMware, Available *at:* https://hostingtribunal.com/blog/cloud-computing-statistics/#gref (Accessed: 12 April 2020)

Mclellan, C. (2019), TechRepublic.com, 'How 5G will transform business', Available at: https://www.techrepublic.com/resource-library/whitepapers/special-report-how-5g-will-transform-business-free-pdf/, (Accessed: 10 December 2019)

Militano, L., Araniti, G., Condoluci, M., Farris. I. and Lera, A. (2015) 'Device-to-Device Communications for 5G Internet of Things', Research article ICST.ORG, 26 Oct. 2015, PP. 1-15, doi: 10.4108/eai.26-10-2015.150598

Puranik, M. (2019) CLOUDTECH, 'How the rise of 5G will disrupt cloud computing as we know it', 19th Aug. 2019, Available at: https://cloudcomputingnews.net/news/?user=22941 (Accessed: 10 April 2020)

Rash, W. (2018), ITWATCH, 'IT Needs to Start Thinking About 5G and Edge Cloud Computing', 7 FEB 2018, Available at: https://uk.pcmag.com/it-watch/93237/it-needs-to-start-thinking-about-5g-and-edge-cloud-computing, (Accessed 19th April 2020).

Rash, W. (2018), PCMag.com 'IT Needs to Start Thinking About 5G and Edge Cloud Computing', 7th Feb. 2018, Available at: https://uk.pcmag.com/it-watch/93237/it-needs-to-start-thinking-about-5g-and-edge-cloud-computing, (Accessed: 04 November 2019)

Roby, K. (2020) TechRepublic.com, '5G promises faster speeds and greater security risks', 23rd Jan. 2020, Available at: https://www.techrepublic.com/meet-the-team/us/karen-roby/, (Accessed: 10 April 2020)

Sanders, J. (2018), TechRepublic.com, '5G mobile networks: An insider's guide', Available at: https://www.techrepublic.com/resource-library/whitepapers/5g-mobile-networks-an-insider-s-guide-free-pdf/, PP. 2-10, (Accessed: 19 October 2019)

Schafer, A. (2019), 'Enhanced Mobile Broadband – 5G Innovation for consumers?', 12th Nov. 2019, Available at: https://developer.qualcomm.com/blog/enhanced-mobile-broadband-5g-innovation-consumers, (Accessed at: 3rd July, 2020)

Shein, E. (2020), TechRepublic.com, 'SaaS, PaaS, IaaS: The differences between each and how to pick the right one', 3rd February 2020, Available at: https://www.techrepublic.com/meet-the-team/us/esther-shein/, (Accessed: 04 February 2020)

Sivakumar, S., Anuratha, V. and Gunasekaran, S. (2017) 'Survey on Integration of Cloud Computing and Internet of Things Using Application Perspective', Available at: www.Mobilenewscwp.co.uk (Accessed: 08 December 2019)

Spall T., Marini C. (2020), IMechEs, 'THE INTERNET OF THINGS IN 2020', Available at: www.imeche.org, Accessed on 18th July 2020.

Talmesio, D. (2018) OVUM, '5G Wireless Home Broadband: A Credible Alternative to Fixed Broadband' Available at: https://www.omdia.com/resources/product-content/5g-wireless-home-broadband, (Accessed: 10 April 2020)

TELEHOUSE.net (2019), 'HOW WILL 5G INTERNET IMPACT THE CLOUD?', 4th Oct. 2019, available: https://www.telehouse.net/resources/blog/october-2019/how-will-5g-internet-impact-the-cloud, (accessed: 17 April, 2020)

Vigliarolo, B. (2020) TechRepublic.com, 'Data security: 5 problems and solutions', 3rd March 2020, Available at: https://www.techrepublic.com/meet-the-team/us/brandon-vigliarolo/, (Accessed: 09 March 2020)

VMWare, Inc. (2016) www.vmware.com, 'BALANCING FREEDOM AND CONTROL: EVOLUTION OF THE CLOUD — 2006–2030', Available at: https://www.vmware.com/radius/wp-content/uploads/2015/08/Balancing-Freedom-and-Control-Evolution-of-the-Cloud.pdf, (Accessed: 07 March 2020)

Whitney, L., (2019) TechRepublic.com, 'How to prevent the top 11 threats in cloud computing' Available at: https://www.techrepublic.com/topic/cloud/ (Accessed: 12 March 2020)

Appendices:

Appendix A: Cloud Frequently Asked Questions (FAQ)

How do I know the level of data security in any cloud environment?

- Your cloud provider should be in a position to provide that information.
- Make sure you ask your cloud provider the right questions regarding security concerns before signing a contract.
- You need to find out what your cloud provider is responsible for and what you are responsible for

When is the best time to migrate to the cloud environment?

- There is no set time to do this. However, by applying the 5Ps, which is **Proper Planning Prevents Poor Performance** this will help make a difference. It is suggested that you apply the phase strategy and proceed sequentially over time. Based on the size of what you wish to move like a database, if it is a small move the whole thing can be done in one go. Based on business experience, start new projects in the cloud going forward.

How do you pay for the cloud services?

- Whatever the cloud model, you are charged according to the level of usage. For example, a non-contractual mobile phone usage, which is pay-as-you-go or pay-as-you-use.

Can an organisation migrate all their business operations and data to the cloud?

- Yes, they could in theory. However, it is not advisable for any organisation or enterprise to do this without doing a proper impact and risks assessment review. The reason being, the risk and cost would be too high. For example, if an enterprise migrates their high priority data over to a public cloud without carrying out an appropriate risk assessment and the cloud environment gets hacked. They could lose their entire business or it may take them a long time to recover from such an incident, if they are lucky.

How do I determine whether or not to store my data in a cloud environment?

- As an organisation determines your business needs and as an individual determine what your personal requirements are.
- As a business what are your goals, objectives and level of achievements you are hoping for?
- Some of your legacy applications may not be suitable to reside in the cloud without making some changes to the system architecture in the cloud, to enable it to work with current services. These changes would add extra costs.
- Migrating to the cloud would require the creation of new operations models and the purchase of new resources and tools in order to manage migration effectively.

How do I determine how much cloud memory is sufficient for my data?

- Your cloud provider is in a position to work this out for you, after you have decided on the data that will be migrated to the cloud.

How do I make sure that my password is safe to use?

- **DO NOT** use your personal password in the workplace.
- **DO NOT** use the same password more than once. If you cannot remember them all, then make use of a password manager to help you.
- Use long passwords that you can remember. Making sure they are made up of alphanumeric, upper case, lower case and special characters.
- For businesses that have moved their data to the cloud, remember to protect your data with strong passwords. **DO NOT** expect the cloud provider to protect them for you. **PLEASE NOTE** - you are responsible for the security of your data and applications.
- Businesses **MUST** ensure they patch their software or applications regularly or without delay, in order to keep them up to date.

How do I determine which volumes of my data to store in the cloud?

- Identify and divide your data into separate groups according to the level of importance or sensitivity.
- It is advisable to keep sensitive data in-house, where you will be more in control and move less sensitive data to the cloud. Especially, when you go for the public cloud option.

How do I determine the best cloud environment for me?

- Once you've determined why you or your organisation wants to use the cloud, then shop around.
- Each of the big providers specialise in public or hybrid computing or both. It is possible to be provided with bespoke or private cloud offerings if required.
- Ask the right or appropriate questions to help you make an informed decision.

How do I protect my information when communicating from an intelligent device via the 5G network?

- By applying data encryption
- Configure multiple authentication access method on the device

How do I confirm whether or not my cloud supplier is a third party?

- Ask your cloud provider. They will be happy to tell you.

How do I confirm the location of where my data is stored?

- Ask your provider, but you cannot do much about it if you go for the public option; as you will not be given the option to choose where your data is stored. As long as your data is available whenever you need it.

In the event of a breach of my cloud environment, who is liable?

- Your cloud provider is liable and this should be spelt out in the service level agreement.
- According to GDPR cloud providers are compelled to report any data compromise within 72 hours of the event taken place to the relevant authorities.

How do I confirm whether the cost of using the cloud environment is reasonable?

- This will depend on what part of your operations will be migrated to the cloud and the level of security of the cloud environment.
- Shop around to determine the environment that is cost-effective for your business.

Is it better to carry out online transactions (e.g. financial transactions) via a mobile device or laptop when using cloud data?

- It would depend on the security facilities provided to protect the cloud environment.
- The devices you are using to access the cloud must be secure.
- Data transactions between your devices and the cloud must be encrypted.

Which companies are the top hybrid cloud providers?

- The table below provides the list of the top companies in 2020. More information on Hybrid cloud computing could be found in chapter two above.

Company Name	Hybrid Cloud	Comments
Microsoft	Windows Azure Pack	Solution is flexible and integrates existing product lines to place it as top hybrid cloud. Holds 17% of global market
Amazon	Amazon Web Services (AWS)	Solution achieved by linking up with partners to provide part of the private cloud. Holds 34% of the global market. Popular with 52% of early-stage users
VMware	Vcloud Air	Specialises in private cloud but relies on partners to deliver a hybrid solution. Shares 36% of the global market with other hybrid cloud providers
Google	Google Cloud platform	Solution depends on vast partner network for his hybrid success. Holds 9% of global market. Popular with 24% of advanced users and only 9% of early-stage users
Rackspace	RackConnect	Solution links organisations private and public clouds. Shares 36% of the global market with other hybrid cloud providers
Hewlett Packard Enterprise	Helion	Solution (i.e. Right Mix) gives customers the option to select percentage of hybrid made up of public and private clouds. Shares 36% of the global market with other hybrid cloud providers
EMC	Virtustream	Rely on partners to provide the public part of the solution. Shares 36% of the global market with other hybrid cloud providers
IBM	Bluemix	Valuable solution due to its open architecture. Provides developer and operations access including catalogue of

Company Name	Hybrid Cloud	Comments
		tools via public cloud. Holds 4% of the global market
Verizon Enterprise	Verizon Cloud	Offers 3 customised cloud plus hybrid solution. Shares 36% of the global market with other hybrid cloud providers
Fujitsu	Fujitsu Hybrid Cloud Services (FHCS)	Solution is a combination of Fujitsu's public S5 cloud & a private cloud. Shares 36% of the global market with other hybrid cloud providers
CenturyLink	CenturyLink's Hybrid Cloud	Delivers public part of the hybrid by integrating with existing systems. Shares 36% of the global market with other hybrid cloud providers
NTT	NTT's Hybrid Cloud	Solution focuses on security and privacy with emphasis on HIPPA, FISMA & PCI compliance. Shares 36% of the global market with other hybrid cloud providers
CISCO	CISCO Intercloud Fabric	Hybrid solutions offered via partner's network. Customer's cloud is integrated with CISCO intercloud fabric. Shares 36% of the global market with other hybrid cloud providers
CSC	AWS	Uses their Agility platform to connect other clouds together. Shares 36% of the global market with other hybrid cloud providers
Hitachi	Vantara	Shares 36% of the global market with other hybrid cloud providers

Amazon provides cloud services for which organisations?

- Apple pays over $30 million for iCloud and other consumer services
- It is estimated that Lyft and Pinterest will pay over $1 billion combined for cloud services in the next few years.

What examples could you give on cloud misconfiguration?

According to (Greg, 2019), they include the following;

- Unsecured data storage elements or containers.
- Unrestricted access to ports and services.
- Excessive permissions, unchanged default credentials and configuration settings.
- Unpatched systems and logging or monitoring left disabled.
- Standard security controls left disabled.

Where could you find the list of companies whose data or environment have been compromised?

- Most data compromises are reported to the Information commissioner's office (ICO) within 72 hours of the event happening. (i.e. https://ico.org.uk/)
- Popular companies data breach list could be found on PRILOCK Security's website (i.e. https://www.prilock.com/breach_list.php)

What is the best viable in-premises cloud storage? (Tech Republic)

- NEXTCLOUD
- OWNCLOUD
- SEAFILE
- PYDIO CELLS
- SYNCTHING

Who benefits from Google Cloud Platform (GCP)?

- GCP is primarily a public cloud provider. Organizations that require cloud computing to improve their business operations either partially or totally will benefit. Especially, Small & Medium-sized Enterprises (SMEs), which the platform was initially geared towards.

What products make up a sample Cloud Platform?

Products	Functionality
Compute	App Engine, Compute Engine, Kubernetes Engine, Cloud Functions
Storage & Databases	Cloud Storage, Cloud Bigtable, Cloud SQL, Cloud Datastore, and more
Networking	Virtual Private Cloud (VPC), Cloud Load Balancing, Network Service Tiers, Cloud Armor, and more
Big Data	BigQuery, Cloud Dataflow, Cloud Dataproc, Cloud Pub/Sub, and more
Cloud AI	Cloud Machine Learning Engine, Cloud TPU, Cloud AutoML, various machine learning APIs
Identity & Security	Cloud Identity, Cloud IAM, Security Key Enforcement, Cloud Security Scanner, Cloud Resource Manager, and more
Management Tools	Stackdriver Overview, Monitoring, Trace, Logging, Debugger, Cloud Console, and more
Developer Tools	Cloud SDK, Container Registry, Container Builder, Cloud Test lab, and more
API Platform and Ecosystems	Maps Platform, API Analytics, API Monetization, Cloud Endpoints, and more
Data Transfer	Transfer Appliance, Cloud Storage Transfer Service, BigQuery Transfer Service
Productivity Tools	Suite, Hire, web browser, Android
Professional Services	Consulting, Technical Account Management, Training, Certification, and more
Internet of Things	Cloud IoT Core

Appendix B: 5G Frequently Asked Questions (FAQ)

Is it secure to use 5G network for sensitive or private data?

- The vision and plan are to provide top-level security facilities in 5G network but this will not guarantee the security of the data's destination or storage location.

What is Augmented Reality or AR?

- Augmented Reality (AR) is a technique where a real world view is augmented, or assisted, by a computer-generated image, this can be in single or multi-sensory modes including auditory, visual, and haptic (NS Final.pdf).

What is Virtual Reality or VR?

- Virtual Reality (VR) is the technology to construct a virtual environment, based on the real environment, within which people can have real-time interactions. There are a number of key technologies used together to enable VR, i.e. 360-degree panorama video, Freeview-point, computer graphics, light fields, etc. Many applications now using VR, for instance; gaming, broadcasting, simulated environments for education, healthcare, military training, etc. (NS Final.pdf).

Which company first introduced virtualization technology and what was the name at the time?

- IBM was the first to introduce virtualisation technology.
- It was called "Time sharing" at the time.
- This was introduced in the early 1960s.

What is Network Slicing in relation to 5G networks?

- Network slicing is the running of multiple logical networks as virtually independent business operations, on a common physical infrastructure in an efficient and economical way. This is a radical change of paradigm compared to current implementations, with network slicing the 5G network is able to adapt to the external environment rather than the other way around (GSMA.com, 2018).

What is a campus network?

- A campus network is a dedicated physical network installed in the premises of an enterprise or organisation. This makes campus networks very flexible (i.e. to build independently of an already existing public network) as they are limited to a small number of devices, which allows the rollout of new hardware fast and efficiently.

Why are Chinese technology companies like Huawei being prevented from working on the 5G network in the United States and Britain's 5G infrastructure?

- There are concerns that any Chinese company given such privilege might lead to vulnerability in national security. In other words, there is a high risk that Huawei might be providing the Chinese government with security information without the knowledge of the countries in question.
- There are concerns that a firm's intellectual property (IP) and patents could also be ex-filtrated from the countries in question (I.e. USA, UK).

Appendix C: Acronym Glossary

Acronym	Meaning
3GPP	3rd Generation Partnership Project
3GPP RAN	Third Generation Partnership Project Radio Access Network
3GPP SA	Third Generation Partnership Project Service & Systems Aspects
4G	4th Generation Mobile Network
5G	5th Generation Mobile Network
5GAA	5G Automotive Association
5G NR	5G New radio
5GC	5G Core Network
ADAS	Advanced Driver-Assistance Systems
AI	Artificial Intelligence
AMF	Access and Mobility Management Function
API	Application Programming Interface
AR	Augmented Reality
BBF	Broadband Forum
BYOD	Bring Your Own Devices
CDMA	Code-Division Multiple Access
CN	Core Network
E2E	End to End
eMBB	Enhanced Mobile Broadband
fog	Extended concept of cloud computing at the network edge
FWA	Fixed-Wireless Access
GSA	Global mobile Supplier Association
GPRS	General Packet Radio Service
GSM	Global System for Mobile
HSPA	High-Speed Packet Access

Acronym	Meaning
ICO	Information commissioner's Office
IMT	International Mobile Telecommunications
ITU	International Telecommunication Union
LTE	Long Term Evolution
mMTC	massive Machine Type Communications
NFV	Network Function Virtualization
NTT	Nippon telegraph and Telephone
QoE	Quality of Experience
QoS	Quality of Service
RAN	Radio Access Network
RFID	Radio-Frequency Identification
ROI	Return on Investment
SDN	Software-Defined Network
SMS	Short Message Service
uRLLC	Ultra-Reliable Low-Latency Communications
UMTS	Universal Mobile Telecommunications System
VR	Virtual Reality
Wi-Fi	Wireless Fidelity

Index:

100Mbps 46, 50
128 bit 51
256-bit key length 51
2G 46, 80
360-degree 102
3D 49, 52
3G 45, 46, 61, 80
4th generation
    network 10
5G
    network ... 1, 9, 10, 11, 13, 15, 44, 45, 46, 47, 48, 49, 50, 51, 52, 53, 54, 56, 57, 58, 60, 61, 62, 63, 64, 66, 67, 68, 70, 71, 72, 73, 74, 75, 77, 78, 80, 81, 82, 83, 85, 87, 88, 89, 95, 102, 103, 104
5th Generation
    5G 9, 10, 44, 104
5th Generation Networks (5G) 44

A

Access 20, 43, 50, 74, 77, 87, 104, 105
accessibility 20
administrators 21
agreement 2, 25, 32, 56, 59, 96
Amazon
    provider 23, 25, 97, 99
Android 101
appendices
    appendix 9, 14, 71
Appendices 91
Apple
    provider 99
Appliance 101
application 20, 23, 26, 35, 59
Application 28, 35, 89, 104
AR 49, 68, 102, 104
Areas 35
Artificial Intelligence 66, 104
Association 104
Attributes 50
auditory 102
automation 28, 49, 52
autonomous 49, 52, 58, 59, 69, 80
AWS
    provider 9, 23, 97, 98

B

bandwidth	27, 45, 46, 48, 49, 52, 75
banned	47
Barriers	38
BigQuery	101
Bigtable	101
book	2, 3, 9, 10, 11, 13, 14, 15, 16, 17, 30, 45, 47, 58, 80, 82, 83, 85
broadband	45, 64, 66, 71, 81, 89
Business	35, 71, 87
businesses	9, 10, 11, 13, 14, 19, 25, 32, 45, 66, 71, 75, 80, 81, 85, 94

C

cameras	43, 53
capability	21, 23, 25, 26, 36, 39, 41, 43, 53, 64, 66, 69, 82
Capability	59
Certification	101
Chinese	47, 103
Cisco	
provider	9
classes	49
cloud	
cloud environment	10, 11, 13, 14, 19, 20, 21, 22, 23, 24, 25, 26, 28, 29, 30, 31, 32, 37, 39, 40, 41, 42, 43, 52, 59, 66, 67, 68, 71, 72, 73, 74, 78, 80, 81, 82, 83, 85, 87, 88, 89, 90, 92, 94, 95, 96, 97, 98, 99, 104
Cloud	
Cloud computing	9, 10, 14, 19, 23, 26, 27, 87
Cloud computing	19
cloudlets	27
Combined	53
Communication capabilities	41
communications	14, 64, 71
commute	53
Compare	28
competitors	15
compromised	14, 99
computing power	19, 46, 71, 75, 78
concept	80, 82, 104
conferences	9
configured	14, 39, 41, 42, 43, 60
congestion	27, 53, 81
Consulting	101
continuity	14
contract	32, 59, 92
Contrast	28
coronavirus	14, 15
Cost Savings	36
Covid-19 pandemic	14
CTO	51
cyber security	9, 10, 14, 38
Cyclic	58

D

data . 9, 10, 13, 14, 17, 19, 20, 21, 22, 23, 24, 26, 30, 31, 35, 36, 37, 38, 39, 41, 42, 43, 46, 47, 50, 51, 52, 54, 56, 58, 59, 64, 66, 68, 71, 72, 74, 75, 77, 80, 85, 92, 94, 95, 96, 99, 102
Data Breaches 30
Data Privacy 37, 42
decommissioned 45
deploying 47
Diagram 22, 23, 25, 29
differences 14, 28, 36, 62, 89
digital 9, 11, 14, 17, 22, 23, 39, 51, 71, 80, 85, 86
disabled 26, 80, 99
Disadvantages 37, 60, 68
driverless 53, 64
dynamic 74

E

efficiency 19, 26, 36, 53
eMBB 49, 51, 58, 104
encompasses 35
encrypted 22, 26, 51, 96
Endpoints 101
Energy Consumption 43
Engine 101
Enhanced Mobile Broadband 49, 52, 89, 104
Enrolment 26
environment ... 10, 14, 17, 19, 20, 21, 22, 23, 25, 26, 30, 31, 32, 36, 37, 39, 40, 41, 42, 43, 56, 59, 68, 71, 72, 78, 80, 85, 92, 94, 95, 96, 99, 102, 103
equipment 36
establishments 22, 23
evolution 4, 46, 81, 86
expectations 45, 46, 47, 50
extremely 49
Extremely 48

F

facilities 14, 25, 37, 41, 43, 61, 82, 83, 96, 102
FAQ 92, 102
firewall 19, 22
Fixed-Wireless Access (FWA) 50
fog 26, 104
Fog or Edge Computing 26
FR1 48
framework 35, 39
Frequency 35, 48, 105
fuel 53
function 31, 35, 45, 56, 59
FWA 50, 51, 76, 104

G

- G model ... 61
- GCP ... 99
- GDPR ... 31, 96
- generations ... 46
- GHz ... 48
- global ... 26, 38, 45, 46, 60, 97, 98
- goals ... 85, 94
- government ... 47, 60, 103
- graphs
  - graphical ... 35
- group ... 45, 51
- guarantee ... 37, 61, 72, 102

H

- Hackers ... 37
- handover ... 50, 72, 74, 76
- Handover ... 50
- handset ... 26, 51
- haptic ... 102
- healthcare ... 68, 75, 102
- High Capital Expenditure ... 61
- highlights ... 28, 47, 49
- History ... 46
- hundreds ... 14
- hybrid ... 23, 24, 71, 87, 95, 97, 98
- IAM ... 101
- IBM
  - provider ... 9, 80, 97, 102

I

- incident ... 93
- independent ... 74, 77, 102
- indirect ... 20
- Inevitably ... 62
- information ... 2, 9, 10, 11, 14, 20, 23, 32, 35, 36, 37, 39, 41, 42, 46, 53, 58, 71, 75, 82, 85, 92, 95, 97, 103
- infrastructure ... 19, 22, 23, 25, 26, 28, 49, 53, 61, 68, 71, 74, 77, 78, 102, 103
- Infrastructure as a Service (IaaS) ... 25
- installed ... 21, 22, 103
- instance ... 36, 51, 64, 81, 102
- integration ... 13, 39, 40, 59, 66, 71, 73, 80, 81, 82
- intelligence ... 23, 25, 49
- internet ... 19, 22, 23, 25, 28, 31, 32, 34, 37, 38, 39, 41, 42, 46, 68, 74, 75, 77, 78, 88, 89
- **Internet of Things**
  - **IoT** ... 1, 9, 10, 11, 33, 36, 80, 81, 87, 88, 89, 101
- Interoperability ... 43
- intruder ... 20
- invention ... 83
- Investment ... 87, 105
- Isolation ... 58

K

knowledge 9, 10, 11, 14, 20, 30, 38, 62, 74, 75, 77, 103

L

Lack of Availability 60
Lack of Backwards Compatibility 61
latency 27, 45, 46, 47, 49, 53, 56, 59, 66, 67, 69, 74, 75, 77, 78
launched 30
leaders 15
legislation 72
level 10, 13, 14, 20, 24, 25, 28, 31, 32, 41, 49, 51, 53, 56, 59, 61, 62, 64, 66, 74, 76, 78, 80, 82, 92, 94, 95, 96, 102
leveraging 81
lightening 64, 71
limitations 10, 27
Limited Storage 37
Lock 31, 88
locked
    locked down 14

M

Maddox 53, 71
magnified 31
management 9, 19, 34, 35, 43, 52, 71, 74, 77
manufacturing 26, 52, 64, 75
market 10, 14, 39, 85, 87, 97, 98
Massive Machine-Type Communications 49, 52
materials 9, 17, 36
memory 37, 46, 94
mergers 31
Message 105
metering 49, 52
microseconds 53
Microsoft
    Provider 24
Middleware 35
millimetre 48, 51
Millions 10
misconfiguration 30, 72, 74, 80, 87, 99
mMTC 49, 51, 58, 105
mobile 9, 10, 11, 17, 19, 20, 26, 37, 45, 46, 49, 51, 52, 56, 58, 61, 68, 72, 75, 89, 92, 96, 104
models 19, 25, 28, 31, 94
Models 22, 23, 25, 29
monitor 31, 36, 59
mortality 83
Multiple 25, 104
multi-tenant 32

N

Nationwide 60
Network 35, 46, 47, 49, 56, 57, 58, 59, 60, 63, 66, 76, 82, 88, 101, 102, 104, 105
Network Slicing 56
New Radio
   NR45
NEXTCLOUD 99
NS 102

O

obsolescence 46
offerings 80, 95
operations 10, 11, 15, 21, 22, 23, 25, 26, 36, 58, 75, 82, 83, 92, 94, 96, 97, 99, 102
operators 47, 56, 82
opportunity 13
organisation 17, 19, 20, 22, 23, 24, 25, 26, 28, 30, 31, 80, 92, 94, 95, 103
organisations 17, 19, 20, 21, 22, 23, 24, 25, 30, 31, 36, 37, 60, 61, 72, 80, 81, 83, 97, 99
outcome 30, 35, 54, 81
OWNCLOUD 99

P

panorama 102
paradigm 49, 102
password 20, 94
percentage 15, 30, 97
Perception 35
Platform 25, 99, 101
Platform as a Service (PaaS) 25
policies 14, 31, 74, 77
possess 31, 52
possession 21
practical 10, 31
precedence 17
Predictive 36, 59
Predictive Maintenance 36
process 10, 23, 35, 36, 50, 74
Processing Power 66
professional 31, 60
professionals 9
properties 2, 47
public 23, 30, 32, 52, 53, 59, 71, 80, 92, 95, 97, 98, 99, 103
purchasing 17, 75
PYDIO CELLS 99

Q

QoS 51, 59, 75, 77, 105
Quality of Service 51, 59, 105
questions 9, 11, 14, 45, 85, 92, 95

R

Term	Pages
readers'	14
Recommendations	85
Reduction	20, 53, 66
References	87
Registry	**101**
Regression	74, 77
research	9, 30, 52, 71, 81, 83
researches	85
Resource allocation	43
responders	53
revenue	20, 21, 78, 81
revolutionise	10, 45, 81, 83
robot	49, 66

S

Term	Pages
Sanders	46, 48, 55, 89
SEAFILE	99
security	9, 10, 13, 14, 17, 19, 20, 22, 26, 28, 31, 34, 37, 38, 41, 43, 47, 50, 51, 56, 58, 59, 61, 68, 71, 72, 74, 75, 77, 80, 81, 85, 86, 87, 89, 92, 94, 96, 98, 99, 102, 103
Security and Issues	72
Security Issues	30, 61
sensitive	23, 31, 38, 49, 95, 102
sensory	35, 102
sharing	36, 102
signs	64, 71
similarities	28
skilled	21, 86
slicing	45, 49, 56, 58, 59, 60, 72, 76, 82, 87, 102
Smart Cities	53
Smart Devices	67
Software as a Service	
saas	25
Software as a Service (SaaS)	25
solutions	9, 13, 19, 56, 60, 76, 78, 89, 98
spectrum	80
statistical	39
Storage capabilities	41
strategy	14, 31, 51, 92
streaming	26, 47, 49, 51, 68
street	53
strike	64, 71
surgery	49, 64
Synchronization	58
SYNCTHING	99
systems	9, 13, 14, 21, 25, 28, 30, 36, 37, 39, 51, 52, 68, 72, 74, 80, 85, 86, 98, 99

T

- table 46, 97
- Talmesio 50, 89
- Team Collaboration 36
- technical
  - non technical 9, 10
- technologies
  - Technology 9, 10, 11, 13, 14, 23, 35, 39, 45, 50, 53, 66, 71, 73, 74, 76, 78, 80, 81, 82, 83, 85, 102
- telecommunication 10, 52, 56
- Telecommunication 46, 105
- telegraph 105
- The IoT 34
- tool 31
- training 61, 85, 102
- transmission 14, 15, 38, 52, 68, 74, 75, 77
- transportation 71, 78, 80

U

- Ultra-Reliable Low-Latency 49, 105
- unauthorised 20, 22, 72
- Universal 105
- Unknown Risks 61
- uRLLC 49, 51, 58, 105
- utilities 60

V

- video 26, 37, 47, 49, 51, 52, 53, 68, 102
- Virtual Reality 68, 102, 105
- virtualisation 26, 45, 102
- VR 49, 58, 68, 102, 105

W

- wave 48, 51
- wireless 35, 45, 50, 53, 58, 64, 71, 75, 77, 87, 89
- world 10, 15, 31, 36, 39, 46, 47, 53, 83, 102

Z

- Zero-Trust Policy 26

www.ingramcontent.com/pod-product-compliance
Lightning Source LLC
Chambersburg PA
CBHW080502220526
45465CB00006B/2350